PENGUIN BOOKS
true fiction

GW00374316

FINANCIAL TIMES
No FT, no comment.

true fiction

A collection of sparkling pieces from the *Weekend FT* column

Edited by Robert Thomson

PENGUIN BOOKS

PENGUIN BOOKS

Published by the Penguin Group
Penguin Books Ltd, 27 Wrights Lane, London W8 5TZ, England
Penguin Putnam Inc., 375 Hudson Street, New York, New York 10014, USA
Penguin Books Australia Ltd, Ringwood, Victoria, Australia
Penguin Books Canada Ltd, 10 Alcorn Avenue, Toronto, Ontario, Canada M4V 3B2
Penguin Books (NZ) Ltd, Private Bag 102902, NSMC, Auckland, New Zealand

Penguin Books Ltd, Registered Offices: Harmondsworth, Middlesex, England

First published 1998
10 9 8 7 6 5 4 3 2 1

Copyright © the Financial Times, 1998
All rights reserved

The moral right of the authors and illustrators has been asserted

Illustrations by Chris Burke, Joe Cummings, Chris Duggan, James Ferguson,
Glyn Goodwin and Matthew Martin.

Set in 11.25/13.5pt Monotype Garamond
Typeset by Rowland Phototypesetting Ltd, Bury St Edmunds, Suffolk
Printed in England by Clays Ltd, St Ives plc

Contents

Preface   ix

Introduction   1

1. The meanness justifies the ends *by Holly Finn*   9
2. I love you trolley, madly, deeply *by Michael Holman*   12
3. Merging on the ridiculous *by Gerard Baker*   17
4. Ready to choose your poison? *by Theodore Dalrymple*   21
5. Rated right off the wall at Blue Moody's
   by Joe Queenan   26
6. The Oz factor in modern thought *by James Morgan*   30
7. Shopping list of a captive spender *by Robert Thomson*   33
8. The 100-year war of words *by Arnie Wilson*   38
9. Under the golden Arch de Triomphe
   by Nicholas Lander   41
10. Marriage on the school syllabus *by Christian Tyler*   46
11. An officer and a gentle man *by Peter Aspden*   50
12. Music to my ears, nose and throat *by Peter Whitehead*   53
13. A fraction short of groovy *by Michael Thompson-Noel*   58

Contents

14. Stealing the signs of the times *by Kieran Cooke*   61
15. Fungi goings-on *by Adrian Michaels*   66
16. Lessons in fretting by numbers *by Robert Thomson*   70
17. The Neanderthals among us *by Christian Tyler*   74
18. When the going gets tough *by Hugh Dickinson*   79
19. Art – it will be the death of us
    by Michael Thompson-Noel   83
20. Boldly gone to a new Enterprise zone
    by Jurek Martin   88
21. Anthony makes his mark *by Paddy Linehan*   91
22. Tallest tales in the shortest stories *by Kieran Cooke*   94
23. Too close to the bone for comfort
    by Nicholas Lander   99
24. A broken heart under African skies
    by Michael Holman   102
25. Pass mark before passport *by James Morgan*   107
26. Character assassination in China *by Robert Thomson*   110
27. The circular route to courtesy *by Peter Whitehead*   113
28. When all else fails, abandon ship *by Kieran Cooke*   118
29. The men with egg on their toes *by Christian Tyler*   122
30. Cartoons to put men in their place
    by Michael Thompson-Noel   127
31. An out-of-court settlement *by Michael Holman*   131
32. When the heat is turned up high *by Robert Thomson*   135
33. When the Angel and the Devil are in the detail
    by Kieran Cooke   139
34. What's bugging the computer? *by Paddy Linehan*   143

Contents

35. Milking the corporate herd *by Peter Whitehead* 146
36. The gentleman vanishes *by Michael Thompson-Noel* 151
37. With my pooter always at the ready *by Kieran Cooke* 155
38. Home of the sporting banana *by Justin Cartwright* 160
39. My search for a sexy messiah
    by Michael Thompson-Noel 163
40. The mother of all inventions *by Robert Thomson* 166
41. A nice girl and her solo number *by Peter Aspden* 171
42. Mischief-making among the particles
    by Paddy Linehan 174
43. Unseemly business in the Vatican *by Kieran Cooke* 178
44. A duty-free shop in every foyer *by James Morgan* 181
45. Become a patron of the arts for 99p *by Peter Aspden* 184
46. Knives out for sharper etiquette *by Holly Finn* 188
47. If that's the question, then what is the answer?
    by Robert Thomson 192
48. A profitable branch of poplar protest
    by Peter Whitehead 197
49. Insights from the sole *by Lesley Downer* 201
50. The stalking octet head for La-la Land
    by Michael Thompson-Noel 204
    The Contributors 209

Preface

Never a truer word was spoken . . . as in true, truer, truest. What you find before you is somewhere between true and truest, the dishonest truth, true faction or, as it is now called by the all-knowing, traction. There will be a fib leaf of truth, and that's a fact.

Genuine thanks to all the unheralded angels at the *Weekend Financial Times* and, for Ping, true love.

ROBERT THOMSON

Special thanks to Anu, Fergs, Peter and Phil.

Introduction

LUC SANTE

What is truth? That question, first memorably posed by Pontius Pilate and later taken up by Johnny Cash ('And the lonely voice of youth asks . . .'), will after centuries of doubt and darkness finally receive a certifiable, binding answer. The European High Commission on Truth, convening this month in Langue-Fourchée (Haute-Savoie), France, is charged with producing a White Paper that will prepare the ground for an exhaustive inquiry, after which ironclad European standards for veracity will be determined. The Commission's spokesperson, Kiri Lavache, admits that the process will not be an easy one. 'Herding into line Italian braggadocio, French Jesuitry, German overstatement and English euphemism is likely to make the standardization of cheeses look like a walk in the park,' she noted with a certain candour. 'And that's merely on the aspect of commercial rhetoric. Just wait until we let in the legal scholars, to say nothing of the military.'

As usual, we can laugh cynically about all of this, imagining the quagmire of definitions, the Babel of cultural misunderstandings, the Talmudic hairsplitting, the stultifying boredom of the sessions, the greenish pallor of the skin of those few delegates arguing arcane points far into the night, the dumbfounding volume of paper produced, the vast ancillary industry of commentators and cryptanalysts required to untangle the Commission's verbiage, and so on. Nevertheless, there will be a report and eventually a set of guidelines, and these will very likely alter all of our lives, for good or ill.

The Commission's mandate is far-reaching: not only is it out to ensure that television newsreaders in every part of the European Union be held to a single standard for reporting frightening or inconvenient developments while avoiding public panic, but also that, say, if you ask a passer-by for directions by car from one hamlet to another in the Bergamasche Alps, he or she will be prevented from resorting to circumlocution under penalty of a stiff fine. No longer will price reductions be described as 'drastic', or soft-drink sizes as 'giant', or subjects of personal ads as 'irresistible'. And, if you are impudent enough to allege to that resistible blind date that you will call him on Saturday, you'd better find someone to feed your cat for the next few weeks.

For those of us in the scribbling trade, the challenges – the dangers – are daunting, and that applies to someone even like me, who does not actually live in Europe, since my books are after all published there. As a popular and freewheeling author of literary journalism, I am often stopped by fans on the street or in the supermarket. 'How did you manage to set down such precise observations of the colour of the sky as you clung to a spar in choppy seas for nineteen days after that terrible shipwreck of which you were the only survivor?' they may ask while proffering the volume in question for an autograph. Or: 'Can you tell me what documentation you unearthed that gave you the exact wording of arguments between the eight year old Sigmund Freud and his mother, as related in your bestselling biography?' Or: 'How is it possible that the space aliens knew enough to invade your home only on those occasions when your wife was away at her mother's?' For some reason, the questions tend to be so lengthy that I have smiled and moved on before they've reached the third clause.

Nevertheless, I am compelled to recognize that I may some day have to answer in court such queries concerning my books, and not just *White Dawn, Beyond Oedipus* and *Pentecost: The Summoning*, but all of the forty-odd titles to which I have asserted my moral right. Understand me well: I have nothing to fear. I naturally applaud the boldness of the Commission's task and recognize the need for its rulings. I am at peace with myself, with my creator and, yes, with my readers. I challenge anyone to disprove the slightest assertion made in any text appearing under my byline. But I am all too aware that, when legalistic bodies apply their sweaty mitts to literature, that most subtle and fragile of human substances, permanent damage may occur. To a bureaucrat, a book is a sheaf of pages filled up with sentences, which convey information approximately the way a coal barge conveys coal. The starched and pressed European commissar, who exists in a world of statistics and bar graphs and actuarial projections and fancy lunches, cannot possibly comprehend the nuances, the shadings, the filigrees – not to mention the blood, the sweat, the tears – that distinguish a work of literature from a report on iron filings or sausage casings turned out by a committee.

I dare say I am prepared to instruct those apparatchiks, if they are willing to listen attentively and not interrupt. I have trod the stony path of literature long enough to have earned a full understanding of the higher truth. In a way, though, I can say that I always knew. My origins were humble, but as a child I was guided by the pole star of reading. Day after day, while my brothers ran around manfully exerting themselves, filching the neighbours' privies and shaking down younger boys for their chocolate bars, I lay on my stomach in the rumpus room and slowly turned pages: Baron Münchausen, Sir John Mandeville, Richard Halliburton – all the great ones. Their winged words transported me to distant lands full of minarets and hippogriffs, lands I knew I would some day visit myself.

I was an indifferent student – a 'dreamer', my teachers all lamented – and so, after graduation from middle school, was unceremoniously apprenticed to the editor of the local bugle. There I laboured seven days a week from dawn far into the night, subsisting on crusts and gizzards, catching my ration of sleep in a discarded milk crate in the cloakroom. Working diligently and without complaint, I found myself slowly but steadily promoted, from errand boy to copy boy to cabin boy to printer's devil to dogsbody. I suffered the abuses of my elders without flinching, knowing that every hurt served the greater glory of the printed word.

One day, when by chance the entire reportorial staff had been laid low by the Anatolian grippe, the city editor, old Schnurr, greeted me in his usual gruff but affectionate way, pinching my earlobe until I sank to my knees. 'There's a package in my vestibule,' he said. 'Get it.' I blinked back tears. I could hardly believe my luck. I realized that I had just been handed the golden opportunity to make my name as a journalist. In a daze, I somehow made my way down the stairs, down the street and through twelve miles of stop-and-go traffic aboard the number seven bus. When I reached Schnurr's impressive mock-Georgian chalet in the outlying suburb familiarly known as Editors' Row, I marshalled my forces. My pocket held the sharpened pencil and the spiral-bound stenographer's notebook that had reposed there unused since my first day on the job. I had my wits, my curiosity and my can-do determination.

I rode into battle. Looking around, I noticed that the bomb squad had not yet arrived and so I decided to begin by way of the servants' entrance. I collared the upstairs maid. 'What was it about the package that aroused your suspicions?' I asked her. She regarded me with bewilderment; evidently she did not speak English. I next spotted the downstairs maid. 'When did you first notice that the package was ticking?' I essayed, a bit daringly since I did not know for sure it was she who had made the discovery. She showed me her back and disappeared. Presumably I had guessed wrong, and she did not want to admit she had not taken the lead.

I had struck out so far, but I knew reversals were common in the trade. I decided to inspect the package, quite possibly risking life or limb in the process. Schnurr's information had been correct. The item sat in the vestibule upon a small gate-leg table under a mirror. It was a cunning job. To the untrained eye it merely looked like a box of clean shirts. Wrapped in brown paper, it bore a laundry stamp; Schnurr's name had been inscribed in a sloping hand. I admired the perspicacity of whoever in the household had been the one to blow the whistle. I approached it delicately, setting each footfall down softly so as not to rattle the mechanism. Gritting my teeth, sweat beading on my forehead, I lowered my head to the height of the package. There was, in point of fact, no ticking. All the more reason for alarm! The bomb therefore had to be composed of some dread dormant plastic substance that gave no outward indication of its menace. When I had mentally weighed and measured the package, and had memorized all of its marks and creases, I beat a hasty but cautious retreat from the hallway. I canvassed the rest of the household. The cook was absent from the kitchen; the parlour was empty of footmen and vassals. Looking out of a window I saw Schnurr's aged mother – the resemblance was striking –

being wheeled away down the opposite sidewalk by the nurse. So the place had been evacuated. I should hardly have been surprised. And, since the nurse had been the last to leave, it stood to reason she had been the one to spot the bomb. She had presumably signalled to the others to flee while she was on the telephone.

The bomb squad still had not materialized. In view of the daring and efficiency of the city's police force, I knew there had to be a reason for the delay. I seemed to remember having once read that certain explosives are all the more dangerous if attempts to defuse them are made too early. It was also more probable that the police wanted to avoid causing a panic in the neighbourhood – that would mean they were waiting until their truck could slip in under cover of night. Matters, then, were in a holding pattern, and there was no more for me to observe. Since time was of the essence and the journey by bus was a long one, I decided to write my story on the way. Sitting in the back row I held my pencil suspended above my pad. There were only two more items to be decided: the assailant's identity and his motive. I considered the range. It was well known that Schnurr had no friends. Logic therefore dictated that he had no enemies either. That greatly narrowed the scope. It seemed unlikely that his mother would be the culprit, since she was too old and feeble to have manufactured the bomb without assistance. Of course, she might have conspired with the servants ... I hesitated. Suddenly the proverbial lightbulb appeared over my head. Of course! It could not be coincidental that the paper's reporters had all contracted a virus that failed to afflict either Schnurr or myself. Like mighty Caesar, Schnurr was the victim of a plot by the very men he had trusted and promoted, whose counsel he had sought, whose fellowship he had enjoyed – if 'fellowship' and 'enjoyed' were indeed the applicable terms. This was nothing less than a *coup d'état*!

I had my story, but as I breathlessly composed it I was stopped short by a sudden thought. I could not bring it to my own paper. The conspirators would make certain it did not run, and then my life would be in grave danger. I knew, however, just what to do. I recast it slightly ('Gazette Editor Victim of Bomb Plot; Own Staff Suspected') and brought it to the rival journal. It took a bit of persuading to get in to see the city editor, Schnurr's old nemesis Plodz, but when the latter had taken a look at the piece he was overjoyed. The story made its debut on the front page of the night-owl edition. It got the whole town talking, and the consequences were swift. The police arrived at Schnurr's house and loaded the package into their wicker truck, where they shredded it – a cautiously worded statement 'could not rule out' an explosive content. The reporters were held for a time and eventually released for lack of evidence, but they remained under enough of a cloud that all of them wound up leaving town. Schnurr took early retirement and he and his mother vanished. Before the year was up the paper, riven by bickering and mutual suspicion among the remaining staff, went belly-up. As for me, I was given a hefty salary and very soon a bi-weekly column by my new employers. In conferring this honour upon me, Plodz emphasized my 'daring to breach the bounds of conventional news-gathering', my 'imaginative willingness to extrapolate from mere wisps of fact'. He noted that I was 'far too unusual a journalist to consign to routine tasks'. My career had suddenly and dramatically been decided.

Since then it has, quite frankly, gone from strength to strength. It is true that I have had my frustrations. No one heeded my advice to look for Martin Bormann on a certain Hollywood back lot, for example – this despite the fact that he is clearly identifiable in crowd scenes in films ranging from *Son of Flubber* to the 1978 remake of *A Star is Born*. Scorn greeted my carefully considered hypothesis that the Soviets had colonized Mars, although some day soon American astronauts will be met by a nasty surprise, those colonists having missed out on *glasnost* and *perestroika*. Even now, few are willing to listen when I tell them of the impending merger between the Mormon church and Shinto, which in turn is merely the first step in a staggering series of planned buy-outs that will before long see the world's great religions reduced to a mere two. But such is the lot of the prophet. In the meantime, I can console myself by casting an eye on my five-foot shelf of bestsellers. Didn't I inform the globe of the value of the grapefruit diet? Wasn't my account of the Kennedy assassination cited as 'definitive' by authorities in several countries? Didn't I give a new hope to millions by revealing the details of the afterlife glimpsed during my near-death experience? Isn't my warning of the coming paradigm shift in mating patterns even now breaking sales records in seventeen languages?

Yes, I welcome the opportunity to testify before the European High Commission on Truth. I will be happy to tell them of all the foregoing, and then I will ask them: Do the learned gentlemen believe that such work as mine can be cranked out by rote, like so many potato pancakes? Can they not imagine a drafting committee composed only of the poet and his muse? Do they not, now and then, look up at the stars and dream? You see, I believe that even bureaucrats contain deep within them something that might be called a soul. Literature is the spark, the balm, the manna that caters to this invisible organ. Its truth is not the dry legume of the bookkeeper, the flavourless broth of the jurist, the hardtack and salt pork of the policeman. Not at all. Its truth, actually, is more like nougat.

1

The meanness justifies the ends

HOLLY FINN *learns how to finish a life sentence*

When I said that Medea was misunderstood, my friend Tom looked at me with great concern and said: You really should see someone. I protested. I wasn't really planning to inject a little cocktail of corrosive fluids into a bottle of Laville Haut Brion and send it anonymously to my ex-beau. And anyway, if I started seeing a therapist, I'd be hooked for years. My psyche would be on one of those never-ending hire-purchase contracts.

Then I heard about END: Efficient Neuroses Diagnosis. The name seemed too neat, too trite, but the idea behind it was compelling.

A year and a half ago, a group of American psychologists, mostly New York-based, banded together and commissioned a market study of their business. The overwhelming response of the 5000-patient survey was that therapy takes too long.

I called Dr Rowan D. Bende, the man behind the movement. He answered his own phone, and told me that, since the study, the group's membership had grown from 15 to 50. 'It's a quiet revolution,' he said. 'You are the first journalist to call me about it.' He was making me feel better already.

'Therapists are starting to give patients not just what they unknowingly want, deep down, but what they say they want as well. We deal directly with the conscious, as well as the unconscious. If exercise machines can give you a flat stomach after six weeks, then we should be able to sort out your head just as quickly.'

Dr Bende admitted that it wouldn't work for everyone: 'It's not for those with machetes in the umbrella stand, you know. If you suffer from multiple personality disorder, we can cope with a maximum of six personalities – seven or more, you should see someone else.'

I liked his sense of humour, so I made an appointment with Dr Bea Leune, who came recommended by Rowan Bende. When I sat on the sofa, buffered by floral-print pillows, she went straight to the point: 'So, what's the time-frame you're after?'

'Two months, maximum,' I said. 'I'm planning a holiday in Cancún for late August and I want to be in a position to relax.'

'Okay, then. How are you?' I noticed that, unlike other therapists I had met, this one brushed her hair. She looked composed, not too brainy, not too flaky, her movements not too jerky and her smile, apparently, natural.

'Well, I'm about a five,' I said. 'On a scale of one to 10. I want to keep believing in *The Sound of Music*, but now the Von Trapps are fighting over their estate and it turns out that Maria wasn't such a peach. And my shoes are ruined.'

'First of all, what the hell are you thinking wearing suede when the weatherman tells you that there is an 80 per cent chance of rain?' She berated me for my fashion sense generally and then encouraged me to talk.

Well, on and on I went, letting out the talkative taxi driver in me. She didn't interrupt until, leaning her leather swivel chair towards me, she said: 'Let's try something.' She started tapping the bridge of my nose. I flinched, but she kept doing it, 10 or 12 taps. Then she leaned back.

'When you do that to people with serious neuroses,' she said, sipping her coffee, 'they blink every time you tap, for as long as you keep doing it. They can't get over the irritation.'

'It is irritating,' I said.

'But a normal person gets over it, creates a logical defence against the intrusion, as they would against people bumping into them on the street, for instance. They deal with it, and stop blinking.'

'And what did I do?' I asked.

'You can open your eyes now,' she said.

I saw Dr Leune for the agreed-upon eight sessions and felt much better. END does seem to change your life by shortening those rambling sentences, you know, the ones that start off with an idea and then seem to lead interestingly on to something else and then encourage you to tell one of those anecdotes that you reminded yourself to memorize because it would surely come in handy some time and you're in the middle of a sentence and you realize that the anecdote's moment has come.

At the end of our last session, Dr Leune told me I was as normal as they come. When I left her office, I realized I was wearing my new pair of suede shoes. It was raining, and I didn't care.

And that was good, very good, because I could really concentrate on the details of the pain I was going to inflict on the beau who betrayed me. Revenge, I chuckled to myself, is a dish best served cured.

2

I love you trolley, madly, deeply

MICHAEL HOLMAN *walked down the aisle – at his local supermarket*

As my Fresh-Picked Herbs brushed against her Cheesey Potato Bake, I thought I was going to faint with pleasure. And when my Linguini came within touching distance of her Fettucine, I had to suppress a groan. I remember it as if it were yesterday, my encounter with the woman I know only as Mixed Salad with Seven Different Types of Leaf.

In retrospect, I overreacted when she produced the item I found so distasteful and which shattered my dream. I haven't given up hope, however, of finding my ideal partner. And so it is that every Friday, at about 7 pm, you can find me pushing a trolley around the food section of Marks and Spencer at Marble Arch.

Some people go to singles' bars in their search for a mate. Others join health clubs, some enlist in dating agencies. Some visit libraries, or tennis clubs or spend afternoons on the down escalator eyeing prospectives on the up escalator.

But I go to Marks and Sparks, for I believe that the search for one's life companion starts with close scrutiny of the contents of their trolley at the check-out counter.

Let me explain. We reveal ourselves through the contents of

our trolleys. Clothes and grooming tend to deceive, but shopping baskets never lie.

What do those of us who do our food shopping at around seven on a Friday evening have in common? We're single professionals and reasonably well off, and tend to leave our weekend shopping until the last minute. And we must be reasonably well off if we can afford rather pricey but high-quality food, using our M&S store card.

And how can you be sure that a shopper is single, I hear you ask? It's simple – the size of the portions they buy tells you whether they have a partner. So I cruise the shelves, pushing my trolley before me, my purchases on display, checking out the Cheese counter, pausing at Pasta, browsing at the Bakery.

I steer clear, however, of Meat and Fish. I once followed an attractive Vegetable Bake and California Seedless Grapes as far as the Smoked Salmon, but my vegetarian sensibilities always prevail. But I digress. It was when I was sauntering past the Salads that I spotted her, a heart-stopping combination of Fresh Squeezed Orange Juice and Dips with Raw Vegetables.

I am fairly sure she did not spot me as I used a ploy that has served me well, before and since. I skilfully manoeuvred my trolley past Cereals, and around Fruit and Vegetables, which allowed me to double back past Desserts.

As I turned the corner, I broke my pace to a casual saunter – though my heart was beating furiously – and came face to face with her trolley, nonchalant as you please.

I hadn't been mistaken. There it lay in a mouth-watering see-through packet: Mixed Salad with Seven Different Types of Leaf. Single shoppers' convention decrees that one does not make a proposition until both parties have cleared the check-out counter.

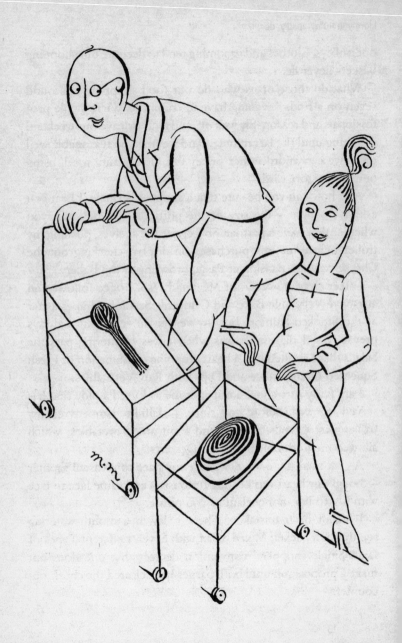

I used to think it a rather silly attitude in this liberated era, but that evening I realized its wisdom, for it saved me from embarrassment, as my story will reveal.

The next step was discreetly to trail the trolley that had won my heart to the check-out, and slip in immediately behind it – a relatively simple stratagem, provided one uses the cover provided by Fresh Cut Flowers.

So there I stood, outer calm concealing inner turmoil, just behind her at the register.

I didn't stare. That would be gauche. But my pulse quickened when I noticed that her basket held several single portions of Cheesey Potato Bake, which happens to be one of my favourites. And there was more to come. It is a list engraved on my heart. A Wholewheat Loaf. Unsalted Butter. A house Chardonnay. Kenya Coffee Beans ('Suitable for Cafetières').

Then came my turn to unload my basket. Only a slip of plastic marked NEXT CUSTOMER PLEASE separated our purchases. Such intimacy, such sweet intimacy.

Do you remember, when you were a teenager, how you would manage to make some accidental contact with the girl you fancied?

Well, it's the same technique in the check-out queue. It was then that I managed to let my packet of Fresh-Picked Herbs brush against her Cheesey Potato Bake, and my heart raced. And when my Green Olives bumped up against her Houmus, I felt like a teenager in the school bicycle shed.

She had Green Beans from Zimbabwe, Fresh Asparagus from Kenya and Cherry Tomatoes from Israel, Macaroni made with Cheddar Cheese . . . I thought I had found the woman of my dreams – until I saw what was at the bottom of the trolley, almost as if she were trying to hide it.

I like to think that I am a tolerant man who would be easy to live with. Had she slipped in a packet of Processed Cheese Slices,

I would still have pressed my suit, although it might have been sensible to have insisted on a pre-nuptial contract.

I would even have set aside my misgivings about Flavoured Mineral Water, provided she agreed that we should test our compatibility by living together before we got married. But I drew the line at Taramásalata. I was younger then, and the years had yet to mellow me.

3

Merging on the ridiculous

GERARD BAKER *sits in on the merger to end all mergers*

D_r Hans-Dietrich Schlepmeister shifted uneasily, noisily in his leather chair as Aaron Z. Vitch III cheerfully crushed another Brazil nut between his jaws, and tackled my question head on.

'Sure, there'll be tensions in the new company. When two great businesses come together in the pursuit of consumer choice and shareholder value, there always are tensions. But think of the synergies!' He thumped the Bauhaus table between the two men, setting Schlepmeister's crystal glass of gently carbonated spring water wobbling.

'We truly are the ideal match, aren't we, Hans-D?' Vitch grinned broadly, revealing an iron foundry where his teeth should have been. His partner watched transfixed, and a little seasick, as his water rolled with each thump of the table.

'This merger merely completes the natural process that began back in the late 1990s,' Vitch continued. 'You remember Daimler–Chrysler, British Airways–American, General Electric and NTT, General Motors and Toyota, Microsoft and Intel. Well, this one's the ultimate example of the integrated economy.'

The global company for the global economy. It was hard to gainsay this message. The merger between the world's two largest companies, announced just minutes before to a packed press conference, broadcast live simultaneously in New York, London, New Delhi, Beijing and Tokyo, had taken even the best-informed journalists and well-breakfasted brokers by surprise.

America Inc and EurAsia AG KK, the world's last two remaining companies, were to merge. America, the information technology-to-fast-food-to-financial-services-to-defence-equipment giant, and EurAsia, the world's transportation, media and heavy industrial conglomerate, had agreed to ditch their long-running rivalry and become a single company, Ameurasia.

With a joint headquarters in Luxembourg and the Cayman Islands, the new company would now provide the ultimate one-stop shop.

Vitch, the son of a building contractor from Brooklyn, who had started out with a lemonade stand in the Dust Bowl, was to be joint chief executive with Schlepmeister, the austere engineering graduate from Cologne who had built EurAsia into the world's second-largest company.

'This is a merger of genuine equals,' the press release had said. 'Mr Vitch and Dr Schlepmeister will co-chair the management board, which will consist of eight other members – seven from America and one from EurAsia.' The stock market had soared on the news of the $15 trillion merger.

Analysts agreed it was the logical culmination of the global consolidation process. The two men had agreed to grant me, as the representative of the world's global newspaper, an exclusive interview. There were many questions.

Would it get through the regulators? 'There are some anti-trust concerns, certainly . . .' Schlepmeister began.

'Oh, didn't you know, Hans-D? We've fixed that already,' said Vitch confidently. 'Our lawyers have been in touch with the authorities in Europe and the US, and they understand the importance of synergy.'

But surely, I offered weakly, the fact that the company will now be the sole supplier of everything to everybody in the entire world must raise some questions from a competition policy standpoint?

'That's the old, outdated way of thinking,' Vitch chuckled. 'The new rules of anti-trust look at the efficiencies to be had from a merger. And in this case, they're pretty big. Customers will get cradle-to-grave service. You'll be able to plug in through Ameurasia's internet networks and order anything you want.'

What about labour issues? Weren't the two companies operating radically different employment policies?

'America is a Right To Work company,' said Vitch. 'And in the present business climate, it's clear that we simply cannot afford the sort of namby-pamby treatment of workers that undermines their self-respect and is growth-negative.' Thump and thump again.

Schlepmeister spoke thoughtfully: 'We have already opened discussions with our workforce about the need for a change and have agreed to a meeting on the subject early next year. I'm confident the works council will agree to the new conditions.'

By that he meant the standard 60-hour week and the replacement of all but a subsistence salary with stock options, traded actively during the lunch break to maximize income. 'Executive remuneration will be less controversial. We have agreed a formula,' said Vitch, who betrayed a satisfied smile.

Then Schlepmeister reached behind his Le Corbusier sofa and pulled out the company's all-important logo. It was a convenient marriage of the two companies' existing motifs. America's size-nine patent leather shoe, symbolizing the march of progress and the triumph of manufacturing, fitted neatly inside EurAsia's legendary Open Mouth of Wonder.

4

Ready to choose your poison?

The world is full of unsuspected hazards, and
THEODORE DALRYMPLE *has identified another*

Now that the scourge of infectious disease has all but been conquered, give or take an epidemic of Aids, Ebola virus and flesh-eating bugs in surgical wards, the greatest threat to our health and well-being must arise from our physical and chemical environment.

For example, it has been conclusively demonstrated – by comparison of the rates of various cancers throughout the world – that 85 per cent of all cancers are caused by carcinogens in the environment. If we wish to live longer, therefore, we must create an environment free of noxious influences.

Chief among these, not surprisingly, are the slow poisons in our food and drink. Heart disease, the biggest cause of death in the western world, is attributable to the western diet. Substances long regarded as innocuous or even healthful may, on closer epidemiological inspection, prove to be deadly. Think of the dairy products which were promoted as being good for you right into the 1960s.

For hundreds of years, mankind has been unknowingly poisoning itself. After all, it took nearly four hundred years to prove that smoking is bad for you. The world, therefore, is full of unsuspected hazards. But there are three important clues to the source of a health scare, clues as obvious to the logician as to the physician:

• The threat should come from an item of consumption of ubiquitous distribution and universal use.

• The illness caused should not have bred contempt through familiarity, but on the contrary should be both rare and devastating enough to produce a frisson of fear in the middle classes.

• The producers of the threatening product, and the government, should credibly (whether they were or not) have been involved in a conspiracy to withhold information from the public, thus permitting an outpouring of righteous indignation.

Is there any item of mass consumption that has not yet been the object of a recent scare? (It should be borne in mind, of course, that no bill of health can ever be final because future research might reveal what past research failed to find.) That item, which until now has escaped suspicion, is tea.

It is indeed strange that this infusion of dried and fermented leaves, known to contain tannin and caffeine among hundreds of other chemicals, which is of very wide consumption, should have gone virtually unnoticed and uncondemned by the epidemiologists and the health pages of our newspapers.

It is surely no coincidence that everyone in Britain drinks tea and that everyone in Britain dies. Tea drinkers have a death rate of 100 per cent.

Research, moreover, has repeatedly demonstrated how dangerous a liquid tea is. For example, when a few drops are added to the water in a tank in which stickleback are breeding, a higher percentage of their offspring than could be expected by chance have a deformation. When the tails of white laboratory mice are immersed in cold tea for three months, 15 per cent of them develop cancer of the skin.

When rabbits, ferrets and guinea-pigs are fed on a diet of tea

EEC Council Directive (10?/6?2/EEC)

TEA SERIOUSLY
DAMAGES HEALTH

through nasogastric tubes, 7 per cent of them develop cancer of the stomach. This experimental research is supported by epidemiological evidence: an examination of the lives of 1847 cases of cancer of the stomach demonstrated that 47 per cent of them had drunk more than five cups of tea a day for 20 years, as against only 26 per cent of those people, matched for age, sex, social class, occupation and so on, who died of something else.

How is it that these facts have so far escaped public notice? Is it not the case that tea is grown and marketed by some of the largest food conglomerates in the country, if not the world? We need look no further: the government, besides raising import duty on tea, is in thrall to the multinationals and dare not offend them.

In short, it has actively suppressed scientific findings, thereby sacrificing the health of the population, to preserve commercial interests.

If tea were not drunk, we should all of us live, on average, 37 minutes longer. Let us therefore forbid the advertising of tea, artistic portrayals (at least in a sympathetic light) of people taking tea, and the serving of tea in hospitals and other places of public resort. Let us demand appropriate health warnings on the packaging of tea, and higher taxes upon the noxious leaf to discourage consumption.

Let us set up a Tea Educational Council to inform people of the dangers of tea (it is addictive, after all) and employ several score of young graduates in psychology and sociology who are at a loose end, but who feel an irresistible urge to serve the public.

Let us aim to reduce national tea consumption by 40 per cent by 2013, and by even more among the specially vulnerable – the old, the weak, the stressed, the tired, the unemployed, the depressed, the pregnant, the young, women, the ill and the middle-aged.

(Adapted from Dr Dalrymple's *Mass Listeria: The Meaning of Health Scares*, André Deutsch, 1998.)

5

Rated right off the wall at Blue Moody's

Music bonds being all the rage, JOE QUEENAN
attempts to cash in

I had just wrapped up the Tom Jones bond rating ($75 million in 10-year notes at 7.8 per cent) when things fell apart completely. I'd been working for six months as a bond rater for Blue Moody's, which had sprung up to fill a yawning expertise gap in the financial services industry when David Bowie and his back catalogue went public, and nobody was sure how to rate the bonds.

I'd already handled Johnny Cash debentures, the Jethro Tull 2009s, and the Mott the Hoople 30-year notes, and had every reason to believe my employers were happy with my work.

With a background in economics and seven years under my belt as a drummer in The Reluctant Gherkins, an early 1970s, pre-post-new wave garage band from Portland, Oregon, I had precisely the kind of arcane, twin-track knowledge of the entertainment world and securities industry that the bond market so desperately needed.

Indeed, Blue Moody's had been founded by two analysts who had seceded from two bond-rating titans precisely because they didn't think their singular expertise was being recognized by their employers.

Gary Krieger had been booted out on the street because he

made too much of a stink about the Gene Vincent 10-year notes, which were terribly undervalued at BAA−, and Chip Lehman was shown the door after he told a tone-deaf boss that Gerry and the Pacemakers, at any rating, was a natural short.

Since I'd already done some work for a Seattle mutual fund specializing in 'Grunge Bonds', the music equivalent of unsecured Third World debt, I was a perfect hire for Gary and Chip.

However, I was the low man on the totem pole, and had to do an awful lot of the grunt work while Gary and Chip hobnobbed with the biggest stars in the business.

When Mick Jagger stopped by the office to discuss a private placement, it was Gary and Chip who got to do lunch. Same deal when Vera Lynn and The Who came calling. That left me in the back office with the dregs of the business. German art-rock bands. Ex-members of The Glitter Band. Back-up musicians from Wham!

I'd like to say right here that I accepted these assignments with the best will in the world. Perhaps my finest moment was when I devised a new bond rating, ABBA, to quantify the risk investors would face in purchasing securities issued by a raft of middle-of-the-road acts from the 1970s. Better examples of the genre got an ABBA+ and the paper to be avoided was rated ABBA−.

But I was also proud of my handling of the Byrds' private placement, which their investment bankers pitched to clients as the Eight Miles High-Income Fund. Fans of the band will appreciate the intricacy of this mezzanine package.

Let me stress that in most of my dealings with rock-star clients I was treated with respect and dignity. The members of Poison were perfect gentlemen with a sound financial base.

Ditto the fund raisers at Iron Maiden and Skid Row. Nor did I have any problems with Black Sabbath in the conduct of their

20-year bond issue, even though there was some messing about afterwards on the secondary market.

No, things went along swimmingly until the afternoon Chip and Gary called me into their office and told me I would be the point man on the bond offering by Head Tundra. Unlike the rest of our clients, who tended to be big stars from the past and could generate income from an extensive back catalogue, Head Tundra was a relatively new band from just outside Swansea who had made just two records.

Though their two CDs – *Scab Scratcher I* and *II* – had sold phenomenally well, there was no way of knowing what the revenue stream would look like ten years down the road. I had seen so many bands like this come and go over the years, and it was my recommendation that the 10-year notes carry a junk rating. Otherwise the bonds were just not going to sell. Alas, my numbers didn't sit well with the band.

One Thursday afternoon, shortly before closing time, the entire group turned up at my apartment. The lead singer, Slime, told me in no uncertain terms that I should run my numbers again.

I explained that the integrity of the firm was at stake, and refused to change them. At this point, the bass player grabbed me from behind, and the rest of the group tied my hands and feet. They threw my furniture out of the window, and I saw no alternative but to upgrade their rating.

Needless to say, the bond offering (5.3 per cent, a mere 20 basis points above US Treasury bonds) found no takers, a misfortune the band laid squarely on my doorstep. When the offering was pulled, I had to change apartment three times and had my car vandalized. Though I have not been able to prove that these crimes were the work of my former clients or their henchmen, it became clear that my life was in danger. Fearing the worst, I decided to leave the US securities industry for ever.

Today, I am working under an assumed identity as a bond analyst for a London outfit called Eighth-Note Securities. We handle ratings on issues like Bach CDs, the *Götterdämmerung* 2050s, Vivaldi's Four Tranches, and Beethoven's Seventh Offering (the Ninth was undersubscribed).

Temperamental they might have been, but these artists are mostly dead, so it doesn't much matter when a private placement is rated middle C.

6

The Oz factor in modern thought

JAMES MORGAN *finds that there is a plot behind an Australian television series*

Astandard joke among my colleagues is the one about the bulletin from the Australian Broadcasting Corporation: 'News just in. The National Library in Canberra has burned down. All three books were destroyed – and two of them hadn't been coloured in yet.'

The British exhibit a malign, almost vindictive attitude towards Australians. They might plead some excuse in the fact that native Australians have often sedulously promoted the unfavourable image that leads inexorably to that quoted above. But many, on the other hand, have tried to rectify the received view by making the world aware of the wide, brown land's cultural achievements which go beyond dwarf-tossing and, I'm sorry, which go beyond some fine films and a star or two of the opera house.

My son was instrumental in ensuring that I became blindingly aware of this fact only the other day. He is a devoted fan of the Australian TV crime series called *Halifax F.P.* which has just ended a run on Channel 5 in Britain. The two letters stand for 'forensic pathologist'.

Halifax is a young woman, forenamed Jane, possessed of comely features and shapely body, and thus fashioned by fate to play a leading role in the adventures of one whose life is spent among the criminally insane. Anyway, in the final episode, Ms Halifax found herself confronted by two Sydney policemen. The boss, a nasty piece of work, was called Derrida. His sidekick, whom he murdered, was Foucault.

I was mightily impressed and promptly called my cousin Rick in Woolamaroo.

He laughed and told me that he had seen the same episode some months earlier while staying with his in-laws. As soon as the two names emerged, his host called from the couch in the lounge, 'Oy, Ethelene, leave the dishes. You won't bloody believe it. They've got a pair of cops named after the grand old man of French deconstructionism and the para-Marxist mastermind of *les événements* of '68.'

I do not know whether every episode of this fascinating series employs such entertaining devices to beguile and puzzle its audience. Did Derrida and Foucault resonate with the plot and its wider societal significance, or was it merely a self-referential *jeu d'esprit*? You won't be surprised to learn that in Australia today there is a weekly panel game on Channel 9 called *Spot the Emblematic Construct*.

This was only one fascinating piece of information to emerge from my e-mails with the Rupe School of Semiotics and Media Discourse at the University of Queensland. Today, this institute concentrates on what are known as 'soaps' by the ignorant but also has time for TV series such as *Halifax F.P.* The Dean, Professor Alan Steinglass, wrote the widely praised study, 'The Hidden Signifiers of *Neighbours*', some years ago.

I found it compulsive reading. In the early episodes of the celebrated 'soap', he notes, there were two characters named Nunn and Miller who married each other. The functionary who officiated at the ceremony was known as 'Priest'. The marriage itself turned out to be both rancorous and Rabelaisian and gave rise to a fruitful chapter in Steinglass's work on what he called 'Chaucerian analogues'.

This area of study does not consist of mere academic speculation: hard-edged politics will intervene in the most surprising way. Readers will recall the last stages of *Dynasty* which in fact prefigured the end of the cold war.

Steinglass says that a KGB double agent from Latvia, Janus Zweigestalt, had penetrated the writing team in order to warn the world of what was going wrong in the Soviet empire. Thus it was that a country known as 'Moldavia' played a major role in the 1988 storyline.

Within two years, Moldavia had emerged from the ashes of the USSR.

Significantly, everybody on the *Dynasty* set said they had never heard of Moldavia. 'Zweigestalt was in fact making a cry for help aimed at anybody who could make the link between the final episodes of both *Dynasty* and communism,' says Steinglass.

Australian viewers have much to look forward to. Channel 9 is now preparing a major series based on a private eye called Roland Barthes who is able to break down all the evidence to prove that in fact nothing happened at all.

The first episode concerns a misleading case of paedophilia entitled Humbert's Echo. My cousin Rick's father-in-law, and all Woolamaroo, will be agitated. 'Oohh mate, an existential counterfactual subsumed in a post-modern canard.'

7

Shopping list of a captive spender

ROBERT THOMSON *is surprised by advertisers' skills in identifying his needs*

Last week, swayed by tempting television offers, I ordered two CDs: a boxed collection of choral classics, and *Velvet Vivaldi*, a selection of excerpts from the composer's more romantic works performed by the London Special Symphony Orchestra – the conductor was unknown to me, but the tunes were familiar enough and the advertiser had skilfully identified my music needs.

A couple of months ago, I rang a TV shopping channel, which is end-to-end advertisements, and bought a machine called Absolute Abs, which promised a firm stomach with not too much effort. I have always been a little unsure about the precise location of my abdomen, but knew I was getting soft around the centre.

From a separate satellite network, I've purchased a set of laminated swap cards of Edwardian novelists, a nest of plastic containers which helped bring order to the fridge, and a six-pack of hair mousse that gives styling stability without the harsh crunchiness of conventional mousse.

For a friend keen on golf, I bought Chip Return, a variation on the old concept of a tennis ball tied with elastic to a brick. I had imagined that a golf ball would be a dangerous projectile on the rebound, but the manufacturer has developed an elastic material capable of bringing the ball to a safe stop. 'From the bunker to the backyard,' is the boast.

By nature, I am an uneasy shopper, with a department-store attention span of around eight minutes.

Yet, at home, I can watch spiel after spiel, channel surfing to catch a once-only offer after watching a unique buying opportunity on another station. And there is the ease of it all – cite a serial code and credit-card details, and you have an imitation leather wallet containing limited-edition stamps of fauna on St Helena.

The most interesting viewing is after midnight, when vending channels seem to experiment with items a little out of the ordinary. My first purchase was a Conversation Starter Kit, which I thought was worth the £29.95 because there definitely are days when I have difficulty forming coherent sentences.

I had presumed that words faltered because of a lack of confidence or concentration, though some friends blame their stumbling on bad biorhythms.

The kit claims to cope with any and every cause. It contains three small ceramic clips, much like alligator clips, which are attached to the end of the tongue and each ear lobe for six minutes.

I'm not sure exactly how it works, but you have a tingling sensation that tells of a gentle current passing through your head.

The problem has not been permanently solved, but you are articulate for about 40 minutes, which is generally all you need to get started most days. Before public speaking engagements or board meetings, I give myself a full 10 minutes of treatment and find an easy eloquence.

I was less optimistic about the efficacy of a gadget advertised very early one Tuesday morning. The inventor was brought on

Essential Home Shopping Kit

Packed With Features

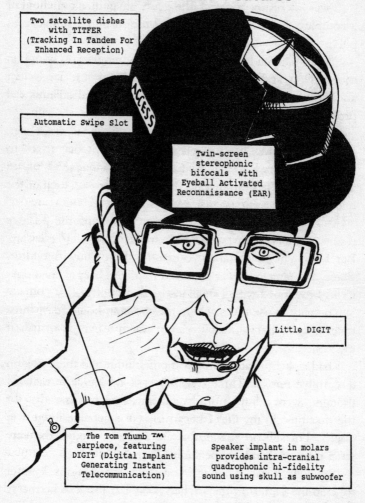

Two satellite dishes with TITFER (Tracking In Tandem For Enhanced Reception)

Automatic Swipe Slot

Twin-screen stereophonic bifocals with Eyeball Activated Reconnaissance (EAR)

Little DIGIT

The Tom Thumb ™ earpiece, featuring DIGIT (Digital Implant Generating Instant Telecommunication)

Speaker implant in molars provides intra-cranial quadrophonic hi-fidelity sound using skull as subwoofer to explain how he was inspired by concerns that his mind was too logical, lacking creativity because the right side of his brain was less developed than the left.

It was interesting to watch the saleswoman then grab hold of a complex, if unoriginal, theory and turn it into a simple sales pitch.

'Think,' she said, 'about the amount of money you spend on moisturizers and after-shave. Now, think for just a moment about your brain.' A few seconds of silence and stillness did prompt reflection on relative neglect.

The machine, the Mind Expander, looks like a bicycle helmet, but, on the inside, has soft plastic suction cups that attach to your skull. There is a small switch at the back that sends pulses in varying patterns through the cups, positioned on each of the main cranial pressure points.

At £79.99, the price was steep for something the positive results of which, if any, would be extremely difficult to measure. But I thought guiltily about ornate bottles of duty-free after-shave, and rang in. It was delivered four days later in an anonymous brown box with a small instruction booklet.

You should use the machine for about an hour a day, three times a week, but you can't read or watch television or talk at the same time.

I had a slight headache after the first hour and there was no discernible impact. Three weeks later, I did perceive that my thoughts were a little more lateral and, after two months, for the first time in my life, I began to take a genuine interest in poetry. I'm still on straightforward sonnets, though the very strict rules of rhyme are beginning to grate.

Last night, I lashed out again on clever contraptions. I prefer to keep the butter on the kitchen table, but that can be messy at the height of summer. A Butter Bonnet (£13.95) works like a car fridge, but has the transparency of a conventional butter holder.

And a Rotaframe (£18.99) appears to be an imitation silver frame, but rotates the photographs on display, much like the moving hoardings at a football stadium. It holds thirty-one photos, so you can have a different snapshot on the mantelpiece each day for a month.

8

The 100-year war of words

ARNIE WILSON *finds his literary mentor is angry at the growing sophistication of language*

Lazarus Woolfson, my literary mentor, becomes unsettled every time a revised dictionary is published. He knows he must yet again acquaint himself with an ever-changing vernacular which he feels is gradually adulterating and trivializing the language from which he has scratched a living as a writer since limping back from Salonika, permanently weakened by malaria, in 1918.

'The language is becoming more and more sophisticated,' he grumbled to me a day or so ago. Of course, he did not mean it as a compliment.

'Sophisticated – derived from sophistry,' he said, as I sat in his gloomy and rather shabby study in London's Grape Street, swigging on my Hooper's Hooch Alcopop. 'In my day it meant adulterated, impure, not genuine. And sophistication was defined as injuring by mixture.'

I did remember something of the sort from my moderate schooling, but even in the pre-Hovercraft days of 1958, this was merely of academic interest.

With the new millennium almost upon us, Larry is particularly anxious. At 96, little short of his personal century, he found the recent attempt by Collins Dictionaries to define the twentieth century in 100 words – using keywords such as suffragette, jazz and girl guide – utterly depressing.

He sought comfort in his first edition (1898) of Chambers – a prize at Mercers' School – for a nostalgic reunion with the language he loved so much he thought it would never desert him. 'Look at this, Arnold,' he barked in a still-resonant baritone. (He is one of the few friends I allow to address me thus.)

'Decilate – another word that has now completed a slipshod transformation. When I started writing after the first war, it meant to take nine-tenths of, or to put to death nine in every ten men. Today's ignoramuses use it to mean something tiny.

'Thank God for the Oxford Dictionary. At least it has the integrity to note that this usage is often frowned upon by careful users of English. But for how much longer? Unfortunately, Thomas Davidson, the editor of my old Chambers, was spot on when he wrote it was not for an editor to judge whether a word was to be added to the treasury of English, "but merely to register such words . . . hence he must admit many words he would not himself use".

'But he would have turned in his grave if he could have seen some of the ghastly words in use today.' Warming to his task, Lazarus leafed through the pages. 'Look at this,' he said. 'Air-space. What d'you think that meant in 1898?' I shrugged.

'I'll tell you: it was the cubic content of a room, hospital ward or the like, with reference to the respirable air in it.' Turning again at random, he alighted on 'orient', a word of many meanings.

Larry focused on the one concerned with adjusting to circumstances and told me it had a sporting origin.

Leyton Orient, the east London football club, had once been a French team called Orient, he explained. During this time, it had been hopelessly unsuccessful, provoking jokes about who put the *'rien'* and 'O' in Orient.

'And this is how we got the word "disoriented".' Trepanning was a surprise too. 'Look,' said Larry. 'It's also from the French: *très* and *panné*. Very broken down. Often applied to the brain. So when they started drilling holes in skulls, it became trepanning.' A word he particularly loved as a young man was contrebulate – something he did often and with a passion. The old Chambers defined it thus: 'To perform, musically, with other or others especially accompanied piano playing.'

Writer, pianist . . . Larry was an accomplished youth. But his talents and enthusiasms were many and varied. He loved equestranavius: 'A game played on horseback on a large squared grid, old English equestrian game played with fence posts in a squared field or area.' He savoured fine food and wine, especially muttock (meat of the chosen lamb) and corley (fermented juice of fruits of the hedgerow).

'I haven't seen or heard of corley for half a century,' said Larry. 'But I believe there are some parts of the world where you can still find muttock – not that I shall be looking, with my digestion shot to bits.' I picked up the great book and alighted on 'blue-stocking' – 'a name given to learned and literary ladies who display their acquirements in a vain and pedantic manner to the neglect of womanly graces'.

'A bit sexist in your day, weren't they, Larry?'

'Sexist?' he harrumphed. 'Another of your ghastly *fin de siècle* words.'

'*Fin de siècle*? Larry,' I said, 'that means the end of the nineteenth century, not the twentieth.' Even mentors occasionally get their come-uppance (orig: hangman's entreaty to the condemned).

9

Under the golden Arch de Triomphe

NICHOLAS LANDER *answers an emergency call in the search for a fast-food fix*

The phone went just after 9 am. I picked it up gingerly. It was either an enthusiastic cold-caller flogging an insurance policy for my video cassette recorder (all repairs covered for the next three years) or another nuisance call from the council about the parking tickets.

'*Bonjour*, Nick. *Ça va?*' I could not place the voice immediately. 'It is Alain Dijon here.' I took a sip from my cappuccino (single estate, specially ground *veluto nero* beans grown at high altitude in the shade) and stammered out a response. It's not every day of the week that I hear from France's, perhaps Europe's, top chef, a man with six Michelin stars to his name.

'I am very well,' he continued, 'business is *très bon*. The new restaurant will open soon. I am at one with myself and my food. The fisherman is feeding sardines to the seagull. But I do need some advice.' I gulped. A French chef seeking advice from an Englishman? Dijon may be cosmopolitan, but even he is fond of telling English food jokes (did you hear the one about the English cook and his native nettle salad?). What could he want? The answer came quickly enough.

'Nick, let me explain. This has nothing to do with my

restaurants but it could be much, much bigger, *plus grand*. Have you got ten minutes?' he asked.

I spilt cappuccino on my trousers and reached for paper and pen.

'About a month ago, I had a call from the marketing director at McDonald's. As you know, *mon frère*, McDonald's is big in France, but they are worried. The burger market is stagnant. Customers are fearful of beef – you know that business at Burger King? And this marketing ploy – the Golden Arch de Triomphe – it has failed.

'And they have other strange ideas, crazy ideas – Maison du McDonald's – it won't work. It is a burger bun without the meat. But they are obsessed. They see the brasseries are packed seven days a week.' I imagined the overnight transformation of McDonald's into places with waiter service and linen napkins. Good for the laundries. Or having to train the counter staff to be testy. 'So, you don't want a drink with your burger and your fries. What is wrong with you? I refuse to take your order. *Merde.*'

'What they want,' Dijon explained, 'is for me to come up with a gourmet gimmick that will turn everyone back to the beefburger.'

'You mean a kind of Burger Rossini,' I interrupted, referring to the composer's innovative slice of foie gras on top of a thick fillet of beef more than a century ago.

'How did you guess?' he replied. I held my silence. I had already noted, privately, that most French chefs like the idea of improving a dish by putting a piece of foie gras on top.

'The slices, they would be easy for portion control,' he continued excitedly, 'and foie gras factories are closing in France so it would help the provincial economy. Even the goose sings when the moon is full.'

CUMMINGS

'Alain,' I replied, 'I am sure you would sell one or two of these McRossini burgers, but that's all – and anyway what about the animal rights groups? They would be barricading every McDonald's in Britain and America within forty-eight hours. What else have you thought of?'

'Well, there are truffles, of course. Not the white ones from Piedmont, naturally. They are successfully growing black truffles commercially, and I'm sure McDonald's could buy them cheaply enough, and you would just sprinkle them (with a little garlic and black pepper) on top of what I imagined could be called the Dijon burger. The flavour, it would just explode in your mouth as you bit into the bun.' I could see this kitchen superstar grinning with gustatory pleasure at his creation.

'Too easy,' I said.

'What do you mean?' he asked. 'It took me days to think of this. The composer does not write his symphony before the continental breakfast.'

'I don't mean too easy to create – just too easy to imitate. After all, it would be a few black pieces of what you and I know is a most expensive ingredient, but it would be too easy for any unscrupulous supplier or server to substitute bits of coloured, diced potato. The name Alain Dijon would be done for.'

'Nick, your wisdom is that of Baudelaire.' Alain sighed, 'I hadn't thought of the sabotage angle. And I suppose you will say the same for my final flourish – a small, round *duxelles* of wild mushrooms which would just fit on the patty.'

'I will,' I said, 'and there are other problems. Most people do not know their *girolles* from their *pieds de moutons* and hardly care. We are talking fast food here, but people need to know that each outlet has personality, charm, character, that certain something.' The line went quiet and I could sense that we were immediately at one.

'Yes, Nick. You are right. The McMichelin Guide. Two stars in Toulouse and three stars at that truck stop near Metz. We will start the tasting tomorrow.'

10

Marriage on the school syllabus

CHRISTIAN TYLER *travels to a rarely visited island which boasts the world's lowest divorce rate*

The marriage customs of Ipotua, a remote island in the South Pacific, are strange. They deserve to be better known. They are not known because visitors to Ipotua are as rare as penguin's teeth. The island has no landing strip, and the traveller must make a long sea crossing. The only hotel, the Shining Surf, is a one-storey building with a tin roof and a total lack of bathrooms en suite.

Despite their primitive plumbing, the Ipotuans regard themselves as sophisticated people. They listen to the BBC World Service and watch the Oscar ceremonies on television. They take in all the news they could possibly need but feel – quite wrongly – they have none to give out in return.

So it was by pure chance that some months ago I saw a report by a Finnish anthropologist which held up the Ipotuan way of marriage as a model for our distracted times.

The system she described was remarkable and in some ways the absolute contrary of western ideas: for example, it seems that Ipotuan couples must go to court in order to get married and can only be divorced following a special conclave of family and friends. I also read that the island had the highest rate of marriage in the world, and the lowest rate of divorce.

So this week, breaking one of my routine tours of Micronesia, I made my way to Ipotua. I was fortunate to secure a room at the Shining Surf Hotel and even more fortunate to arrange a meeting with His Excellency Chief Henry Margana, the island's registrar-general of marriages.

I found the chief sitting on the verandah of his office, a breeze-block edifice from whose palm-covered roof the blue, white and red flag of Ipotua fluttered listlessly in the humid air. Over the door was a handpainted sign: 'Marriage is our business.' The chief followed my gaze, saying as he shook my hand: 'Just so, mister. Margana is my name, marriage is my game. Welcome to Ipotua.' He beamed.

I thanked him for finding the time to see me, and came straight to the point. 'Surely,' I said, 'marriage is none of the state's business. It's a personal matter.'

'So your Mr Blair says. I heard him yesterday on the BBC. But still he wants happy families. Here we say, sure, sex is for grown-ups. But marriage is for parents and their children, our children. So of course we are interested.

'On the other hand, like your Mr Blair, we are short of money,' the chief went on. 'The government of Ipotua does not have the means to bring up children and keep them out of trouble. Also, we are too busy – governing, and fishing, and so on,' he added vaguely.

He explained that the island's children were given sex education at home but marriage training at school. If, having passed their marriage exams and having left school, they wanted to get hitched and so enjoy the considerable tax perks that an Ipotuan marriage confers, they had to go before a tribunal for intensive questioning in order to secure a licence.

'What about love?' I asked.

'What about it?' replied the chief. 'It depends what you mean by love. Anyway, that's none of our business. Marriage is our business,' he added irritatingly.

I remarked that it seemed a cold-blooded process.

'Look,' replied the chief, clasping his big hands together. 'The state cannot make young couples happy. But it can give them a damn good chance.'

'You mean they go into marriage with their eyes open?'

'Yes. As Chancellor More said: "Would you buy a colt without looking for saddle sores?"' It was an odd analogy coming from a man who had probably never seen a horse.

Nor, for the life of me, could I remember a chancellor of that name. My face must have betrayed my bewilderment, for the chief went on: 'About four hundred and fifty years ago your chancellor Thomas More visited a country like ours. I have his book in my office.' He jerked a thumb behind him. 'In that country, men and women were shown naked to each other before marriage, so there was no complaining they didn't know what they were in for. Same here. Once you buy, we don't want to take goods back. *Caveat emptor.*' The chief grinned triumphantly.

Beginning to feel the heat, I asked: 'Why, then, does your tribunal not also grant divorces?'

'Does the tribunal know the couple? Does it know the children? No,' the chief replied. 'The families and friends know and the families want to protect the children. Besides,' he added slyly, 'it is not so easy to divorce if you have to face the friends and relations.' Taking pity on my ignorance, the registrar-general went on to explain that marriage was getting tougher all the time. Even in Ipotua, he said, women were no longer so dependent on men, nor so forgiving of their waywardness and weakness. Television and advertising had encouraged everybody to 'paddle their own canoe', to please themselves before thinking of others.

The chief took a credit card out of his pocket and waved it under my nose.

'You see, mister. Pleasure now, but pain later. Here in Ipotua, if you want the pleasure of marrying, you must have credit in the bank.'

'Credit?'

'Wisdom. In here,' said the chief, tapping the side of his head.

I was beginning to tire of His Excellency's easy confidence about a problem which had defeated the best brains in the western industrialized world. So I asked him how long he had been married.

'Not married, mister.'

'May I ask why not?' The registrar-general leaned forward and winked heavily:

'Still in training,' he said.

11

An officer and a gentle man

Having survived boot camp, PETER ASPDEN *went manoeuvring in the military*

I, at least, lasted longer than Riddick Bowe. The former heavyweight boxing champion who had always dreamed of a life in the military managed just eleven days in the US Marine Corps Reserve before throwing in a towel with barely a bead of sweat on it.

Bowe 'could not handle the regimented-training lifestyle', which proves that all that business in Rocky films about half a dozen raw eggs and a jog at five in the morning was as fanciful as it was stomach-churning.

But I am hewn from a different block of medium density fibre. My experiences with the military, thus far kept in an X-file deep in the bowels of London, offer a sharply contrasting fable of fortitude. I took the boot camp in my stride, as it were. The training was a joy. I got on fine with the boys, there was mutual respect. By the end of our time together, there were tears.

The key to my success was in allowing them, as they say in Santa Monica, their own personal space. They were all tougher, meaner, badder – I knew that. There was no use in my coming over all macho and trying to compete on their level. I offered them something different. Call it a chance to communicate with their feminine side or perhaps with their innermost being. They lapped it up. For they had never encountered a Regimental Intellectual before.

I decided on my approach from the first day, when I turned up in Louche Velvet Dressing-gown when the script demanded Full Metal Jacket. There were laughs, of course. But I was ready for that. They barked out orders: 'Bombs away', or some such pithy piece of urgency. I countered with the aphorisms of Lichtenberg: 'I am extraordinarily susceptible to loud noises, but they lose all their disagreeableness as soon as they are connected with some rational objective.' They went curiously silent, but were impressed.

I pointed out to them fundamental mistakes in their strategy: for example, the use of heavy metal music to flush out the enemy in sieges, as perfected in 'Mad' Maxwell Thurman's tactics against General Noriega in Panama in 1989.

Would they not be much more effective playing the Alanis Morissette album over and over again? Tests proved me right. It was a matter of subtlety, I explained. For the Army to use heavy metal was too much of a muchness, whereas it was well known that nothing rotted the mind like dippy teenage feminist revenge soft rock. They had never even heard of her, bless them.

Soon, I began to organize small encounter groups within the regiment to discuss issues like these. We even made up a name – Effective Fighting Forces Evolving Towards Enlightenment – but the authorities became mildly concerned that we were undermining morale.

I soon convinced them, however, in a secret meeting held in a virtual reality helicopter in a games arcade. Armies had nothing to do any more, I said. The war was over. History was over. There was no point at all in boot camps, drill, manic physical exercise, all those savage chants, when there was no enemy any more.

Furthermore – and this was the clincher – if you could prove that life in the Army helped you become a complete, fully-rounded human being, Lichtenberg aphorisms and all, might there not be a compelling argument for the reintroduction of national service? Their eyes lit up. They saw unemployment figures diving into a sea of nothingness, while their reputations soared into the stratosphere. The authorities can be a tough nut to crack, but give them a tantalizing flash of a knighthood and they become pussycats.

That is how close I came to changing the public life of this country. But it was not to be. They lost their nerve, said they couldn't live with the PR implications, and muttered something about the Falklands and national pride. They began to infiltrate our George Eliot seminars, sabotage our aromatherapy sessions, and pour axle grease into our flotation tanks. All my initiatives were frustrated.

I decided to leave with dignity intact. Not for me the Riddick Bowe way, slinking away sheepishly. I wore my sparkling white ceremonial uniform and swept into the mess hall. The music swelled, eyes moistened. I picked up my books, my energy crystals, my aphorisms and strode out purposefully.

There was applause, I cannot deny it. And I could not resist a final dig: how the officers blanched when I told them that their army was, after all, no place for a gentleman.

12

Music to my ears, nose and throat

There is no cure for the common cold – but
PETER WHITEHEAD *finds we may not need one*

Eating an orange does you no harm – it might even do you some good. But, as a cold remedy, middle C beats vitamin C nearly every time.

As scientists pack away their pipettes, satisfied that there is no possibility of a cure for the common cold, a new generation of healing hands is searching elsewhere, working on prevention and relief of symptoms.

The new kids in the lab believe there is no need for a total cure; the common cold consists solely of symptoms, and a cold without symptoms is therefore no cold at all. And it's where the cutting edge of medical research meets old wives' tales that is proving most fruitful.

At the forefront is that old playground joke – What do you call a boy with a runny nose and no handkerchief? Greensleeves! The young things in white coats have studied the genealogy of this punchline and made a promising discovery: Henry VIII's favourite tune has been found, in repeated clinical tests, to possess profound therapeutic qualities.

The healing power of music was well known in Henry's time and beyond. From the sixteenth century on, *Greensleeves*, and other popular tunes, were hummed and strummed to cold sufferers to relieve their symptoms. But then, around the middle of the 1800s, doctors ridiculed the practice, calling it mythical, and so it ceased.

Since then, the focus has shifted towards prevention, most notably the eating of oranges. But what the experts have also found is that oranges are not all of one type.

Miniature oranges are a prime example. The vitamin C from each type is slightly different and has varying preventative qualities. Thus, satsumas do nothing to prevent a tickly throat, but can fend off a blocked nose – the nasal nerve endings are toughened up by the gushing quantities of vitamin $C-3/PO$ in a satsuma.

Clementines, rich in vitamin $C-BR600$, can, in most people, keep that tickle at bay. The chest is made more resistant to coughs and catarrh by tangerines, while mandarins (the sort you can peel with one hand) keep sinuses in good shape. Ask your greengrocer which is which.

Several laboratories in Europe and North America are conducting parallel studies. I learned this from Corey Cross, the youthful head of the COLD Discovery Unit at the Communicable Virus Control Institute in Placerville (aka Old Hangtown), California.

'Colds are great business in California. We have entire departments in most stores devoted wholly to cold remedies. Even people without colds take stuff – no one wants to get one,' he explained.

'But what we can do now is work on prevention, where fruit and sensible precautions are important. And, if that fails, we attack symptoms with exactly the right remedies.

'Steam, vapours, honey, lemon, drugs, they're all OK for a couple of hours.

'A bellyful of alcohol and curry is better – though you usually

regret it the next day.' But only music had any real effect on the symptoms, his team found. If a song or symphony is in harmony with an individual's biorhythms, it is the number one all-round symptom-buster.

'It's the oldest remedy in the book but unused for a hundred and fifty years, because a few influential doctors found it odd. We are now having to debunk the myth that debunked the old wives' tale,' Cross said.

As someone who once suffered a cold lasting fifty weeks – it began on 8 August 1996 in the upstairs bar of London's Vaudeville Theatre – I begged to know more. How do people catch colds? 'Enclosed spaces,' he replied. 'Lifts, aeroplanes, doctors' surgeries, offices. Don't go near them during the cold season. A germ from a cough or sneeze can live in a warm, sealed environment for up to ten hours, ample time for it to have made thirty laps around an office air-conditioning system.

'The next quickest way to catch a cold,' he said, 'is to venture outside in winter with wet hair – it lowers the resistance to almost everything.'

On the positive side, Cross is sure that the right selection of music means the cold war is almost won. The final nail in its coffin could be a simple test his unit has devised that can identify which tunes work best for each person.

I asked if I could try the test which will be available to doctors early next year. A small package arrived from California. I was to take it to my GP, who would administer the test.

Apart from the forty-five hazardous minutes spent in the waiting room with what sounded like a dozen bronchial patients (I held my breath), the operation was painless: eighteen micro-needles attached to a palm-sized computer extracted tiny blood and tissue samples. The results could be read in seconds.

The computer said I was category P8715/W1913. For cold

prevention I should drink blackcurrant juice and, as a catch-all multi-symptom suppressant, I needed a stiff dose of loud Welsh rock music. I left the surgery with a prescription for three Manic Street Preachers' CDs, to be played very loudly and often at the first sign of a sniffle.

And so far, so good. My state of health has been so transformed that I can sometimes go to work, and without my constant companion, the handy packet of throat lozenges. I must recommend it to the neighbours – they seem to have been suffering from headaches and, surely, prevention is better than cure.

13

A fraction short of groovy

MICHAEL THOMPSON-NOEL *tries to make it into Miss Lee's bonobo society*

I was in a high-class coffee dive in Beirut the other day, twaddling away an hour, when, by coincidence, in swept Miss Lee, my erstwhile executive assistant, accompanied by a gang of young male sports stars. There were two South American soccer players with really big hair, a Lebanese pentathlete, a Canadian weightlifter, two Czech swimmers, and so on. They looked as fit as fleas and all – this was clear – were in thrall to Miss Lee.

When she was my assistant Miss Lee ruled my life with the truculence you would expect of a glamorous, Thatcherite Yorkshirewoman, though these days our paths seldom cross. ('Thatcherite' is a portmanteau word. It is often wielded as a pejorative, though in Britain and elsewhere many people use it as a synonym for numerous sterling qualities. In relation to Miss Lee, I employ it in the specialized sense of 'Iron Maiden in a John Galliano frock'.)

'Hiya, Miss Lee,' I said, waving a hand at her gang of athletes. 'I know you like muscles, but this is ridiculous.' She said: 'You never change, Michael. But try to be cool or you'll be out of your depth. Between them, these 15 boys own 17 world sports titles and 16 world records. But they're not just testosterone.

They are charming and intelligent. And all of them, Michael, are employed by my foundation.'

'Foundation?' I queried weakly, swirling my cappuccino. 'Here in Beirut?'

'Here, there and everywhere,' responded Miss Lee. 'My foundation is thoroughly international and abundantly well endowed. We're here for a seminar. Tomorrow we'll be gone. Moscow, as it happens, for a chat with President Gaga.' It was dawning on me that things were changing fast in the life of Miss Lee, so I adopted a tone that I often employ, one of faux-befuddlement.

'I've lost it,' I said. 'What are you doing here with fifteen muscle guys? What does your foundation do?' Miss Lee fiddled with the emerald bracelet she always wears, and motioned to one of the Czech swimmers to bring her an espresso.

'Put it like this,' she said. 'The universe is 15 billion to 20 billion years old, yet most of its lifetime – 100 billion years? 900 billion years? – is still in front of it.

'Thanks to capitalism, there are no limits to what humans might achieve in that time. This is because there are no limits to the wealth humans might create. With no limits to wealth, there can be no limits to our exploration and colonization of distant galaxies.

'Correction, there is one thing that limits the creation of wealth: human male aggression. Human males are a tragic holdover from our species' rainforest past. So we're eliminating most of them. Governments and significant corporations everywhere want this to happen.

'As a result, very large sums have been awarded to my foundation, which is leading the campaign. Soon, the human species will boast a female-to-male ratio of 49 to 1. How is your primatology, Michael? Ever heard of bonobos? From now on, humans are going to behave like bonobos.'

'Oh, sure,' I said, 'bonobos.' I straightened my Herbie Frogg tie and told the Canadian weightlifter to refresh my cappuccino. He did not bat an eyelash. Hardly even looked at me. I could have been an ashtray.

'How about this, Miss Lee: of the five species of ape, two – gorillas and orang-utans – are fairly violent, and two – chimpanzees and humans – are ceaselessly violent. In the jargon of primatologists, male chimps and humans are demonic males.

'But the fifth ape species, bonobos, who were formerly and mistakenly categorized as pygmy chimpanzees, are wonderfully peaceful and gentle. In bonobo society, females hold the power. To maintain order, they gang up on the males. Bash them around. Quite possibly, the suppression of violence among males in bonobo society has also led to the suppression of all predatory aggression.

'So, if humans were like bonobos there would be no genocide, warfare, rape, assault – just harmony and lots of sex. And if you've set your sights on a human female-to-male ratio of 49 to 1, it's not surprising you're collecting groovy male athletes.'

'Not just athletes,' said Miss Lee. 'I am also in the market for a few creative and artistic males.'

'How about me?' I said. 'I'm a Piscean, Miss Lee. That's why I'm such a dream-boat. Chopin's birthday is 22 February. Handel's birthday is 23 February. Mine is 24 February.'

'Michael,' said Miss Lee, '49 to 1 is a cruel ratio. If it had been 49 to $1\frac{1}{32}$ you might have squeaked in. But it isn't. So you won't. It's the age-old story, sweetie: a miss is as good as a mile.'

14

Stealing the signs of the times

The English village is under attack. KIERAN COOKE
reports on damage limitation

Up till last week, locals in the village of Upper Warble would recall only two events in recent times which had threatened the peace and harmony of their Cotswold community. In 1923 an over-enthusiastic campanologist dislodged the great bell on St Ailred's church, causing it to crash through the roof of the nave, injuring himself and the vicar.

Colonel Philpott de la Strange, returning to the Manor House after the Second World War, decided his wife had been liaising too closely with the estate taxidermist. In his highly emotional state – compounded by the lingering after-effects of malaria – the Colonel put a torch to the Lutyens-designed house before taking out his parang (a Malay sword) and destroying one of the finest topiary collections in the country.

But, last Wednesday morning, Upper Warble awoke to find things had taken a sinister turn. In the space of a few overnight hours, all the hanging baskets which had decorated every porch and lamp-post in the village had vanished. The neighbouring hamlets of Chipping Warble and Warble-on-the-Water reported similar disappearances.

More than a hundred such decorative objects had gone missing – numerous road signs, and the 'Welcome to the Warbles' banner (sewn by the local Women's Institute), which had been removed from its moorings. Julian Smith-Fluster, a derivatives trader who chairs the Warble parish council, warned of the arrival of urban vandals in rural areas.

There were hints that neighbouring communities, jealous of Upper Warble's 1998 'Most Pretty Village' award, might be responsible for the mysterious disappearances.

'Our heritage will not be stolen from us,' Smith-Fluster told a packed village hall. 'We will have our baskets and signs. The Warbles will never be beaten.' Sitting at the back of the meeting, I could not resist a wry smile. It is our small but dedicated band which is responsible for the Warbles' distress.

It is all in a good cause. Put simply, our mission is to stop the prettification of England. The Warbles were chosen as the starting point for this grand and noble project.

Arthur McCoy, a man of impeccable rural credentials (he is a specialist on nineteenth-century silage techniques), is one of the moving forces behind our group. Writing in a recent issue of the *Pig Breeders' Gazette*, he eloquently put our case.

'England is becoming a theme park,' said McCoy. 'Prettification threatens to strangle the life out of our communities. Villages are neat, smug and lifeless. They are no longer for living in but, like Babylonian brothels, meant only for visiting.' McCoy, who takes on the appearance of an over-ripe tomato when his passions are aroused, painted a dire picture of the future. 'Before too long we village dwellers will be expected to carry hanging baskets down the street with us. We will have to wear special costumes. Those of us considered unsuitable for the tourists to gaze upon will be told to stay indoors.

'Wholesome rural odours will be outlawed. The baaing of sheep and mooing of cows will be forbidden. The plan is that,

village by village, our stealthy raiders will venture out to remove and destroy every hanging basket in the country. Window boxes will be smashed. Flowers will be returned to the wild. Future generations will thank us for our endeavours.'

The other target of our noble campaign is the road sign. At a time when rural libraries are being closed and most villages have to survive on one bus a month, some mad bureaucrat has decided to spend millions littering the country's verges with a bewildering range of ugly iron posts and lettering.

In Upper Warble (pop. 46) there are now four sets of 30 mph markers and three sets of 40 mph posts. There are also five dead-end and nine cul-de-sac signs.

A notice by a ploughed field warns of falling rocks, while a series of fresh signs by the disused railway track warns drivers of locomotives.

There is more of this idiocy outside the village. One sign directs the traveller to the scenic route, the starting point of which is a quarry.

Another, beside a bunch of stinging nettles, tells of Upper Warble in bloom.

Worst of all is the ten-foot display a mile down the road with the message 'You are now entering Shakespeare's County'.

Contrast this with the position in Ireland, happily blessed with a paucity of signposts. While many visitors might be wandering around wondering where they are for most of the time (a coachload of nuns from Bruges left Dublin for Kerry in late August and has not been seen since), few seem to be adversely affected. After all, being lost – impossible in today's England – can be an enriching experience.

In one daring overnight raid, our gallant band successfully liberated the Warbles of all these ugly objects. We now move on to the rest of the country. Hanging baskets and road signs will be turned into ploughshares.

Hopefully, England will never be the same again.

15

Fungi goings-on

ADRIAN MICHAELS *puts store on the unknown efficacy of the mushroom*

It started with the mushrooms. Four hundred and forty pounds of porcini mushrooms to be precise. Porcini mushrooms come in fancy packets, dried and strongly flavoured. On the trendy dinner-party circuit they appear in wild mushroom risottos and the like.

Robert Oldman had seen only a handful of packets in his life. At the small supermarket he managed in an unfashionable suburb in south London, there wasn't much call for such exotica. If he sold a packet, the wonders of modern stock control meant that computers at area warehouses sent him another, and that was that.

He was very impressed with the store's new point-of-sale electronic scanning equipment which could read smart chips attached to each item in his store.

Combined with store loyalty cards, individual customers' buying habits could be tracked. And the company also knew at any moment whether Oldman was running out of medium-slice white loaves. Or cat litter. Or tinned tomatoes. And it would send him some.

But last Tuesday he was confronted with a loading bay stacked high with, the packets assured him, desiccated fungi from the most select woodland areas of northern Umbria.

According to the delivery paperwork, Oldman had sold 8000 packets of porcini mushrooms in the previous three trading days – yet his store hardly stocked any desiccated fungi. He headed back to his office to make some unsavoury phone calls.

But someone at the warehouse had already been trying to get hold of him. On his telephone message system, an agitated voice demanded to know what he was doing selling so many porcini mushrooms. By the way, the caller inquired, why had this store sold no other product in the past 72 hours?

At check-out till 23, the nearest to his office, Oldman watched an elderly woman sliding bananas, carrots, tinned pineapple, dog food, a carton of milk, a loaf of bread and 12 toilet rolls on to the conveyor belt. As the smart chip attached to each item rumbled past an electronic eye, the till flashed up a message: 'Beep. Mushrooms, porcini, Euros 5.60. Beep. Mushrooms, porcini, Euros 5.60. Beep. Mushrooms, porcini, Euros 5.60 . . .'

He raced out. Till 22: 'Beep. Mushrooms, porcini . . .'

Oldman wheeled round. Till 21: 'Beep. Mushrooms, porcini, Euros 5.60.' Till 20, till 19, till 18. All the same.

'This is a customer and staff announcement,' a breathless Oldman shouted into the intercom. 'Everyone leave the store. Bomb alert. Go home. Leave the store.'

By 3 pm, every supermarket in the country had closed down, except for one near Sloane Square where no one seemed to find the vast sales of upmarket mycelia at all odd. A national emergency was in full swing.

Technicians were frantically examining the smart chips on groceries and trying to reconfigure them. But every scan was the same. Every chip persisted in holding the same message. Every supermarket product thought it was a desiccated fungus from northern Umbria.

Theories were demanded. One scientist told the BBC on

Wednesday that smart chips, which have recently replaced the older bar codes, emit magnetic fields. In very high concentrations, on the shelves of supermarkets, for example, those fields could become confused.

Was it possible, even, that the chips on the vegetables had become sentient? Had they just taken the single currency one stage further and opted for the single price? The single good? It seemed patent nonsense but no one was going to pass up the opportunity for hysteria. And there were headlines to be written.

'We are the champignons', roared one tabloid on Thursday morning, while a weightier broadsheet informed its readers that they were 'Living in a persistent vegetative state'.

And then, later on Thursday, came a breakthrough. An isolated banana placed in a lead-lined room was having its chip interrogated by a team of scientists. The conviction that it was a mushroom began to waver, the chip first announcing that it was a porcini banana costing Euros 40.

Finally, the chip relented and decided that it was, after all, a banana.

Distanced from its fellow groceries, it had lost whatever magnetic stimulus had caused it to rebel.

The supermarkets were relieved, but shopping is expected to change for ever. It has been found to be too dangerous to stock items close to each other. Experiments discovered that they must be at least 1.6 metres apart.

Land prices around supermarkets are already soaring as the bigger chains plan to build over areas as large as small towns. Shoppers will have to walk vast distances simply to fill a basket.

Smaller shopkeepers are rubbing their hands. Unencumbered by new technology, they are able to offer chip-free shopping in its older, more sedate form.

But in a bid to attract the ultra-chic, cutting-edge buyer, some supermarkets are using the new technology in a different way. They are deliberately stacking smart-chipped goods too closely together.

After all, there is nothing more certain to impress a dinner party than the appearance, late in the meal, of a small platter of monstrously expensive porcini bananas.

16

Lessons in fretting by numbers

ROBERT THOMSON *comes face to face with fengshui*

Off a cobblestone lane, down a narrow alleyway, along a darkened corridor, the fifth door on the right and then the third door on the left, there is a small house within a house, its archway entrance decorated with a red banner. As I stand on the threshold, gathering thoughts and contemplating whether to take the next step, a gentle voice comes from inside the building: 'Please do not hesitate, you are welcome.'

Thin plumes rise slowly from incense sticks in an earthenware pot behind a bare wooden table and the only light is cast by a candle that flickers, but does not melt wax, as it burns. 'I know why you have come.' Only a face is illuminated, an ageless north Asian countenance, but I cannot tell whether it is man or woman, and the voice, with its haunting reassurance, is beyond gender.

The moment I enter the vacuum of indecision, the voice is calming: 'For your sake, not for my understanding, explain the predicament.'

'My troubles began many years ago as a teenager,' I said, 'when watching a television programme, *Kung Fu*, about a shaven-headed monk on a spiritual passage through the American wild west.

'At first, it was an undergraduate joke on the railway platform:

"Grasshopper, when a train is late, it will be followed closely by many like-minded trains." I gradually became fascinated by fengshui, making sure that my first apartment was not on a T-intersection, putting a large mirror on the rear wall to reflect negative energies, and buying a collection of kitsch wind-chimes, which remained silent in my airless rooms.

'"What is it with T-intersections?" a doubting friend asked, when I made a partial confession a few drinks into a long dinner. Sobering for a moment, I explained that the spirits flow up the stem of the T, straight into homes on the corner. "Like a sozzled lorry driver?" he giggled.

'That was my last public confession. Then came a concern and, later, an obsession with numbers, in particular the number four. I had read that Chinese avoid it because *si* sounds like death and I noticed on a business trip to Taiwan that my hotel didn't have a fourth floor. The elevator went straight from three to five.

'I have not watched Channel 4 for six years and skip page four of most newspapers, presuming that it will be full of pestilence or unbearably grim court cases. When I play golf, driving from the tee – I know it's a different word – but I shout "eight", which I'm told is *ba* in Chinese, close to *fa* and prosperity.

'Everything from buying shoes, which must have fewer or more than four holes for laces, to entertaining at home, where I never have dinner for four, is determined by the numbers. I like the occasional flutter on the horses, but refuse to punt on race four, and suffer a strange coldness in theatres at the mention of "fourscore years . . ."' My muse was unmoved. There was the gentlest of smiles, knowing, not mocking.

'And your office desk, which had four drawers?'

'Yes,' I admitted, 'it now has three.' The most intimate of my secrets was known, the most extreme of my fears.

'You must understand that fengshui is a fashion, not because it is written about by gurus of lifestyle in *Wallpaper* magazine, but because it has existed for only 3872 years.'

'You are sure about that date?' I asked.

The smile broadened: 'A provocative question. A farmer on a hillside overlooking a clear lake in what is now Shandong province in China's north was trying to sell his shack, having decided to move south to escape barbarian attack. From this most basic of transactions, the folklore of fengshui was spun.

' "Nice view," the potential purchaser conceded. "Much more than a nice view, the spirits are on your side," countered the confident farmer. "Think of this as a buying opportunity not only for your successors, but, more important, for your ancestors." The farmer then told of the auspicious winds blowing across the hill to the waters below, and explained how he had found this prime location with the assistance of a bamboo divination stick.

'The purchaser was impressed by the conviction in the farmer's voice, but said that he was looking for something larger. "Three rooms are not really enough for my wife and two children, we need four rooms." The farmer frowned and then slowly shook his head: "Forgive me, brother, you said four rooms. I can't believe that you would want to condemn your family to misery in this life and even more misery in the nether world. Four is the most ill-fated of numbers. It is cursed. Three is altogether more lucky.'

My muse did not need to finish the story – I looked down at my slip-on shoes and felt foolish. As I was leaving, there came one last piece of sage advice: 'Have fun with fengshui.' And so I have.

In my spare time, I have written a book, *Four Things You Didn't Know about Fengshui*, still to find a publisher. And I am working on the sequel, *Neo-geomancy in the Nineties.* There are tips on knife and fork arrangement, on curtain colour co-ordination, playing poker to win, and on what to do with wind-chimes in airless rooms.

17

The Neanderthals among us

CHRISTIAN TYLER

Some things that come in the post you just know are going to be good even before you open them. That's how it was with the plain brown envelope which fell on my desk this week.

We recipients of leaked documents can be too ready to believe what's in them – we are flattered to be chosen. Here, we think to ourselves, are deep secrets of state, matters of grave public interest which the anonymous donor has entrusted to the most responsible scribbler in the trade – to wit, me.

This time, however, it was immediately obvious that the stuff was dynamite – obvious, too, why the government should have decided to suppress it. The photocopied memorandum of an unnamed official was attached to the bundle. It said it all: 'I cannot stress too strongly that public security and community relations could be severely disrupted were this research to be published' (I liked that mandarin subjunctive), 'not to mention the criminal justice system, employee recruitment, the insurance industry and who knows what else.' Let us go back a bit.

For many years, mountaineers in the Himalayas and trekkers in the American far west have reported sighting large hairy hominids, or have photographed their footprints. There is a lively traffic in tales of the Yeti, Susquatch and 'Big Foot'. The people engaged in it are usually dismissed as nutters. I should make clear that the documents on my desk did not actually refer to such creatures. But what they implied was more bizarre still.

You will be aware of a long-running controversy in palaeo-anthropology between those who say homo sapiens is descended from Neanderthal Man, and those who say he is not. Most scientists today regard the two brands of homo as separate species, even though they seem to have cohabited in Europe for about 10,000 years, up to about 25,000 BC.

Poor old Neanderthal Man, so the story goes, did his best to keep up: chopping flints, throwing spears, nibbling pistachios, cooking over pine-branches. But, despite a more than adequate brain (up to 1600 cubic centimetres), he could not get his mind round new technology quickly enough, and was gradually driven to the fringes of the Continent – to places such as Gibraltar – where he expired.

Others say that his poor, brutish wife may well have fancied baby-faced sapiens (because he looked so much like her own infants) and may even have got him into bed. But their union could never be fruitful: for they were different species.

Doubts persisted, however. And now, in front of me, was the report of a molecular biologist from a government-funded laboratory (all names had been removed) claiming to show that DNA had been successfully extracted from a skeleton of homo neanderthalensis and shown to match the genes of some modern humans.

In other words, to put it crudely, there are Neanderthalers walking among us today.

When I revealed this scoop to friends, they seemed unsurprised. 'I've always thought so,' was the common reaction. These sophisticates have not considered the implications.

If some of us are Neanderthalers, very soon we will want to know who is, and who is not.

Neander is German for New Man. But you can bet no sensible woman would want to marry one. Employers will be demanding genetic tests – would you knowingly employ a Neander if you could get a Sapiens? Insurers will demand higher premiums. Eventually, there will have to be equal opportunities' tribunals, special Neander counselling parlours. The British government will feel obliged to run Neanders-only shortlists for parliamentary constituencies.

The legal implications are horrific. What will the judge say when defence counsel offer Neander genes in mitigation? No doubt, though, that football clubs will want a few playing in defence.

Worst of all will be the confusion out there on the street. Appearances, we know, are deceptive. Just because he looks tough doesn't mean Sylvester Stallone is a Neander. I would say his sensitivity puts him firmly among the Saps. The same goes, obviously, for the wonderful, witty Muhammad Ali. Is Arnold Schwarzenegger one? No, he's far too clever at pretending to be dumb.

Cary Grant, on the other hand, was a consummate Sapiens impostor.

Go back in history and you will quickly realize that Beethoven was one, where Mozart was obviously not. Indeed, it is now clear that the Romantic movement as a whole was a Neanderthal revolution.

The trouble is that Neanders were forced by natural selection to be good mimics. You have to look at the DNA to be sure. Only the most maladapted failed to insinuate themselves into polite society and were left picking berries in the Himalayas or the American forest.

I made one copy of the laboratory report. Yesterday it vanished from my desk while I was out. I am afraid I suspect the colleague who shares this office: he is always insisting on humankind's insurmountably apeish nature.

The original, I hand-delivered to a top palaeobiologist, a Fellow of the Royal Society, no less, for his confirmation. Too late I realized that he, too, could be one.

I may never see that paper again. And, without the evidence, who will believe my story? Neanderthalers apart, that is.

18

When the going gets tough

HUGH DICKINSON *believes his travelling companion is getting too close for comfort*

'This is a speed-restricted area,' murmured Hillary in her husky voice. I should have felt grateful, but was irritated. I knew it was. Her close attention to my every move was getting on my nerves.

I'd had a choice at the car rental office: male or female voice in the inboard computer. 'Hillary' or 'Bill'? On balance, I thought I'd prefer a female companion on the long drive up to Vermont. The mechanic showed me how to reprogram the black box under the dashboard.

'She can tell you in different ways,' he said. 'Some folks don't fancy a particular tone of voice.' I soon found out what he meant. I'd hardly got the key in the ignition before Hillary started to tell me how it was.

'Fix your seat belt,' she commanded in a flat Yankee voice. 'Adjust your rearview. Release your handbrake.' Negotiating the manic Boston traffic is nightmare enough for a visitor, but driving with a built-in New England schoolmarm reduced me to a sweating sponge. I pulled into the first filling station, unlocked the black box and tried to remember the codes I had been told back at the rental office.

Despairingly, I pushed a few buttons and drove on. The result was delightful. Hillary's voice had dropped from a peremptory twang to a soothing southern drawl.

'I guess you-all may want to check the gas,' she murmured. I glanced down. 'Thanks,' I said. 'My pleasure,' she husked. Startled, I looked at the empty seat beside me. We had coded in my destination four hundred miles away at the office, so I wasn't too surprised when Hillary gave me advance warning of a turn-off on to the Interstate. She did it, well, so suggestively.

But I objected when she proposed turning off twenty miles on. 'Hey, we're heading for Vermont, not Chicago. You got your wires crossed!'

'Only a suggestion,' she reassured me, 'but there's a big tailback up ahead and I thought maybe we'd take a route round it. But you're the boss.'

'Okay, okay. You just tell me where to go.'

'Sure, that's why you hired me.' With gentle precision Hillary guided me through the back streets of a small town and back on to the Interstate twelve miles north. On the southbound side, the traffic was stacked up for miles.

'That was brilliant!' I exclaimed as we sped up the empty road.

'Thanks,' said Hillary, 'my pleasure.' And then, 'Maybe we should watch our speed here, folks.'

'Why's that?'

'Cops ahead and a speed trap.'

I eased off and we floated past the waiting police cars as demurely as a maiden aunt.

'Good thinking, Hillary.'

'I sure wouldn't want you-all to get tangled with those Yankee cops,' she said.

Hillary was a winner. I pictured her, a slim blonde with long, brown legs and green eyes. She interrupted my day dream.

'Sorry, no. Brunette, with glasses and built kinda square.' I jumped and stammered an apology.

'That's okay, it often happens. But it's my voice you hired.' And your personality, I thought. There was a distinct chuckle. I began to feel nervous. And hungry. 'If you-all are feeling like a bite, there's a place a mile west at the next junction.'

A prickle ran down my spine. Hillary was reading my mind. Over a monster beefburger and a can of root beer, I reflected. This recoded Hillary was getting a bit too close for comfort. I had a map in the trunk of the car. If I switched her off I could map-read the rest of my route.

I went back to the car and put the key in the door. It wouldn't turn. I tried the trunk. The same. I was locked out. As I leant my head against the car I heard that husky chuckle again. This was ridiculous. I gave in. 'Okay, you win.' The key turned in the lock. I opened the door and then slipped back to the trunk. It wouldn't budge. Without a map, I would be lost in the winding mountain tracks of Vermont.

'Promise you won't switch me off?' I sat behind the wheel and thought of game plans to outwit her. On every one she was ahead of me, and gently explained her countermove. We drove on.

The root beer was trickling down to its final destination and the need for a comfort stop pushed all other thoughts from my mind.

'Men,' snickered Hillary. 'Only one focus to their lives.' She sighed. 'Take two rights and there's a shopping area 200 yards down with a Sizzler on the corner. That do?'

'Fine,' I said. Fine it was. Beside the Sizzler there was a branch office of same firm that had rented me the car. I slipped in and asked if they could change the vehicle for me – brakes fading a bit, I explained glibly. They couldn't have been more obliging.

The mechanic lifted my bags out of the blue car and into a nearby black one.

He started to explain about the black box. Did I want 'Bill' or 'Hillary'?

'Can you switch the thing off?' I asked nervously.

'Why sure – just pull this lead out.'

'You jerk!' whispered Hillary with sudden venom.

The mechanic looked at me with his mouth open. Cheerfully, I did just what Hillary told me and jerked the lead out. And, boy, did I get myself lost on those mountain roads. Pathetic, really.

19

Art – it will be the death of us all

A doomsday installation is missing. MICHAEL
THOMPSON-NOEL *needs a volunteer to find it*

It packed them in. But the Sensation exhibition at
London's Royal Academy, showing controversial works by young
British artists, was not my scene at all. It was tosh, mostly:
dead-end art, witless huggermuggery – a thought which must
haunt the man from whose collection the works were loaned,
the notorious Charles Saatchi.

I, on the other hand, operate in a realm of the art scene so
rarefied that when I gaze down on people like Saatchi, it is as
though an eagle were observing an ant.

Because of my knowledge of art and my degree in quantum
physics, I am an adviser to the true titans of the international
cultural scene – the multibillionaire patrons of doomsday installation art.

There are five of them. I cannot tell you their names. One
lives in America, one in China, one in Australia, one in Iceland
and one in England – in Herefordshire, actually.

That is all I can say about them.

Instead, I will tell you about doomsday installation art, which
is tricky stuff. I did not realize how tricky it was until this week
when Mr X (I have to call him that) summoned me to his
Herefordshire estate.

He sounded panicky. Mr X is one of the five international titan-patrons of doomsday installation art. Originally, advised by me, Mr X was a big-time investor in sporting works. His Herefordshire estate is dotted with such installations, including a basketball court, an 18-hole golf course and a full-size replica of the Centre Court at Wimbledon.

These are not sports facilities. They are works of art, expensive to install and maintain. The Wimbledon installation, for example, shows a stick-thin figure representing Tim Henman, the British player, battling ineffectually against a sinister, faceless, granite-muscled opponent.

The work is entitled Droopy Drawers Drops Another Set, and is insured for £75 million.

But the aesthetics of sporting installation art are limited, and even the unutterable plangency of Droopy Drawers Drops Another Set cannot rescue the genre from banality.

So, to steer Mr X towards the cutting edge of postmodernism, I introduced him, three years ago, to doomsday installation art, which spotlights the various threats to the survival of mankind.

These include: nuclear, biological or chemical warfare, destruction of the ozone layer, the greenhouse effect, a new Black Death, asteroids and comets, a nearby supernova, 'green scum' or 'grey goo', catastrophes arising from mishaps with genetic engineering or nanotechnology, computer-related disasters, annihilation by extra-terrestrials, and so on.

Mr X and the other four patrons of doomsday installation art had been planning to create a series of doomsday artparks around the world, to show mankind how close to extinction it really is. The first park was due to open next July.

But now there is a problem.

When I was helicoptered to Herefordshire this week, Mr X

greeted me at the helipad. He is only four feet tall, but he drives his Aston Martin with élan.

As we sped across the park towards his stately home, Mr X pointed out the doomsday installations of which he is especially proud. They include the mile-wide Green Scum Lake, which is revolting, Black Death Strikes The Sydney Olympics, which is horrific, and Bill And Hillary Are Not From This Galaxy, which shows the White House being run by extra-terrestrials.

But Mr X's most expensive doomsday installation is the one that is causing problems. It is not installed in the park. It is housed in his gymnasium. Or, rather, it was, because this work of art, entitled Eternity Is Made Of This, has disappeared.

Theoretically, Eternity Is Made Of This is a small black hole. It was made by applying inestimably large pressures to a can of baked beans, so that the can collapsed endlessly, creating an unimaginably small black hole which then re-expanded to occupy its own hyper-space – its own tiny universe.

Now Eternity Is Made Of This has disappeared.

'Why is that a problem?' I asked Mr X. 'I thought Eternity Is Made Of This was saying something ironic about the futility of human scientific adventurousness in the face of our near-certain extinction some day soon. It cost $3 billion to manufacture, so its disappearance is triumphantly futile and ironic.'

'That is correct,' said Mr X. 'But now the maths underlying Eternity Is Made Of This have been recalculated. And the outlook is dire. According to the new sums, Eternity Is Made Of This was always bound to pop out of existence for a short while.

'But it is due to pop back into existence in 2008, in the form of a very large black hole that will swallow us all. And there you have the irony. We are not going to be killed by science. We are going to be killed by art.'

'That's OK,' I said. 'It is the ultimate proof that doomsday installation art has intellectual underpinnings, which is more than can be said for the Sensation exhibition at the Royal Academy.'

'But what should I do?' implored Mr X.

'I'll speak to Charles Saatchi,' I said. 'I'll convince Charles that he will become the most famous man in art history if he lets us beam him down the tunnel of time in pursuit of Eternity Is Made Of This. When he meets it, there will be a wonderful explosion that will prevent your artwork from rematerializing in 2008, or on any prior or subsequent occasion.'

'But that would be the end of Charles Saatchi,' said Mr X.

'What a great day for art,' I said.

20

Boldly gone to a new Enterprise zone

JUREK MARTIN

As my old friend, Kermit, used to sing, 'It's not easy being green.' And he was just a frog on a children's television programme. It's far worse, believe me, if you're a real alien, not just some kind of immigrant being harassed at airports because you look foreign, but a genuine bona fide creature from what you earthlings call outer space.

I know because I'm one. Actually, if you're interested, I don't have many problems at national borders because I can reassemble myself in any form known to man – and a few others you could not even guess at. Also, you learn from experience, like not trying to get into Britain disguised as a dog, which I'll tell you about some other time.

What's really got my goat – and what brings Kermit back to mind – is this new book I heard about and ordered through the IBS (the intergalactic bookshop). Its point was that *Star Trek* was, from its beginning in the 1960s and in all its many subsequent manifestations, a vehicle for the promulgation of racial and sexual discrimination.

Now I know this can't be true because I've been on the bridge of the Enterprise more times than I've had hot dinners. Mostly I was hitching rides from one planet to another, but Kirk never knew I was there because his scanners and sensors could never pick me up. I was, if you like, a fly on the wall – a disassembled collection of super-atomic particles would be more accurate – and there was nothing I missed, not even the Romulan brandy if they left the bottle open in the wardroom.

I won't deny there was something a little pat about the composition of the Enterprisecrew. Yes, Kirk was a white American male, as was McCoy, the doctor, while Spock, his number two, was half-Vulcan and therefore some kind of superhuman being, viz the Vulcan mind meld – a useful technique, though crude by my standards.

But it was slightly ahead of its time, even for the 1960s, to have a black woman, Uhura, as communications officer, and a Russian and an Asian allowed to fly the Enterprise when the cold war was at its height and Japan still only made third-rate Toyotas. And the joke character was a Scotsman – a nice touch.

But they had the sort of humanistic values that I, as a post-postmodernist even then, rather liked. A lot of Klingons did get zapped and phased, but violence, à la Quentin Tarantino, was normally the last resort, not the first, and the Klingons asked for it most of the time. They just needed a bit of acculturation, as the social scientists now call it.

And Kirk and his crew did accept that some of those aliens (i.e. me, if they'd known I was there) were of a higher intelligence, worth trying to understand. I mean Kirk even tried to reason with the Gorn, a pretty offensive kind of giant lizard from another galaxy whom I'd once tried to civilize, and then refused to kill him after knocking him out with a home-made gun.

But this, I now read in this new book, was all a smokescreen, hiding the facts that Kirk, a notorious lecher, drew the line at chatting up Uhura and that the Klingons wore black hats as a metaphor for not giving them actual black skins. And one of the nastier villains, Khan, used to be an Asian warlord during the Eugenics Wars at the turn of the third millennium when he could just as well have been Caucasian, like, say, Thatcher in her second coming, as your history books will reveal.

And no woman gets anything other than a supporting role, mostly supporting Kirk in the sack. Spock had no interest in sex, which is not surprising given that Vulcan sexual mores forced his father to marry a human.

Some of the later series have changed this a bit, even with a woman starship commander, but I put that down to the political correctness that had become prevalent.

I'm not against affirmative action. We have similar laws in our intergalactic federation which have worked well, though our lawyers – and what a picky, overpaid lot they can be – and our politicians are forever trying to take the guts out of them. But, then, we've got seventeen defined sexes and people of every size, shape and colour, which doesn't count the genetically engineered chameleons, so our problems are a little bit more complicated, as we discovered when we introduced our common currency, the quark, and then had to replace it with gold.

No, my real problem with this book is it does not understand the demands of travel in space and time. After all, the mission statement of the Enterprise was to boldly go where no man has gone before, which is pretty noble if you forget the split infinitive and which, by and large, was fulfilled. This meant that Kirk and his crew became creatures of space, not earth. I know you cannot remove all recidivist tendencies (like sex and race) but, what with being transported at warp speed and with all the anti-matter flying about and the transponders up, the shields down and the phasers on stun, they never had much time to dwell on them. Believe me, I know, I've been there.

21

Anthony makes his mark

If Noah had been a Ricky, would he have bothered with the Ark, asks PADDY LINEHAN

People become their names. Penelope has always been prissy and Bartholomew a bachelor, while Bob and Robert are never the same person. There are researchers who have devoted their lives to explaining the intricacies of eponomology, and yet the significance of their work has been condemned to obscure journals and poorly attended seminars.

One of the most profound case studies was that undertaken in 1991 by Professor Richard Ferdinand, of Cambridge University, into the name Elizabeth. He recorded the significant differences in behaviour of the same girl who was called successively Betty, Lizzy, Liz and, then, Elizabeth.

Betty was rather boring, while Lizzy was hyperactive, gossipy and, ultimately, prescribed a six-month course of anti-depressants.

The professor's work was reviewed favourably in the *Quarterly Journal of Eponomology* and received a one-paragraph mention in the *New Scientist*. But his ideas were gathering dust until he was contacted a couple of weeks ago by a member of the Prime Minister's staff, who explained that Tony Blair would like him to visit Downing Street to discuss the science of names.

The meeting was informal. 'Shall I call you Dick,' Blair asked. 'I'm sorry, Prime Minister, I really am a Richard. And I have long suspected, sir, if I may say, that you are an Anthony. The "Tony" is just political populism, I presume.' Blair's doe eyes lit up and he smiled a toothy, slightly embarrassed smile.

'Yes, yes. I refused to allow my schoolmates to call me Tony or Tone. I told them I was born Anthony and would always be Anthony. But then one must make compromises in politics.' The teeth flashed again and he tossed his head back as would a starlet or as one would looking for cobwebs in the corner of the room.

The Prime Minister then began to speak seriously, and somewhat drearily, about a New Britain in which every man, woman and child would have the name they deserve, a name which would enable all to achieve their full potential.

He explained his plans for a small renaming project in London's troubled Tower Hamlets: 'I think that young Gary, now a glue-sniffer, will be a truly brilliant student as long as we call him Ralph.' In the future, the first phase of the welfare-to-work programme would be a change of name for the long-term unemployed.

Ferdinand said the Prime Minister was wise to place his trust in name determinism: 'Take Adam and Eve, they didn't have a chance. These were not random choices by the Bible writers – with names like that they were bound to eat the apple. Now, if Adam had been Sebastian and Eve had been Edwina, the history of mankind would have to be rewritten.'

The professor was keen to prove that history was with Anthony Blair: 'Take the account of the flood. What would have happened if Noah had been Ricky? Would we have survived the flood? Would Ricky have taken the time and care to build the boat that saved mankind?' Without waiting, he answered himself.

'No, Ricky is no boat builder . . . Ricky is a surfer.'

Convinced, the Prime Minister formed a sub-committee which

he asked the professor to chair, and called for a list of new-era names to be compiled. A spin doctor dropped in on the committee's first meeting, suggested that this new welfare programme be called Name Your Future, and provided a few 'winner' names: Alastair and Albert (never Al) were on the A-list.

There would be good Christian names such as Matthew and Simon and Theresa and a few cultured names culled from the European continent: Pierre, Pablo, Gunther and Vaclav. Not a loser among them. Welfare namers would be sent out into the jails, and Butch and Kev would no longer be 'lifers', prisoners of childhood names that led them inevitably to crime.

Women, too, would be rehabilitated. Veronica and Deborah (even Debs would be allowed in certain circumstances) were two names highlighted by the committee for use by hardened crims like Moll and Jill. (Out of respect for the Prime Minister and his wife, Anthony and Cherie would be on a restricted list.)

The Prime Minister was moved by the committee's vision. He burst into an impromptu speech, all the more compelling for its unnaturally long pauses: 'It is time to become a representative democracy . . . Inherited title has no place in the New Britain . . . We all have the right to a name that will guarantee us, and our country, a safe, secure, prosperous future.'

He stopped speaking – although, because of the strange pauses, it wasn't clear for a few minutes that he had finished. Then he exhorted the committee to press on. Once the names of existing under-achievers were changed, and most social problems effectively dealt with, the committee must oversee the naming of the newborn. It would be a dream fulfilled: state support from cradle to grave.

22

Tallest tales in the shortest stories

Skip the headlines and scour the littlest items on your paper's inside pages, says KIERAN COOKE

The world is full of surprises. Take, for instance, the strange and no doubt terrifying experience of Melanie Thompson. Ms Thompson works on a checkout counter at a Co-op supermarket in Lancashire.

One day recently, as she stabbed her fingers at the till, totalling up the baked beans, heads of cauliflower and strings of sausages, she was overcome by a peculiar sensation.

Ms Thompson's knickers had spontaneously combusted. Imagine the commotion as the unfortunate worker moved to douse the flames. She was left with scarred buttocks. A fire officer was unable to explain the incident.

The headlines might talk of tumbling stock markets and celebrities frolicking on Mediterranean yachts. These lavishly told stories pass me by. Instead I head for the few lines at the bottom of an inside page that tell a more personal story. Some call it trivia: but these small details of human existence are my obsession.

Such tales do not have to be comic. Some are tragic. What's important is that the imagination must be challenged and the spirit revived.

Not long ago, I was lying in hospital recuperating from a stomach operation.

Hidden away beneath talk of Bill, Boris, Tony and the rest of the gang was an item concerning the travails of an English country publican and his family.

The family had decided to go on a caravan tour of France. At the last minute Grandma, 84, said she would like to come along.

On arrival at Folkestone it was discovered that Granny did not have her passport, or any other form of identification. The landlord refused to contemplate making the arduous journey back down the motorway.

Granny was told to hop into the caravan and hide herself till the party had arrived in France. On arrival, the caravan door was opened and there was Grandma, dead.

The landlord decided to make a clean breast of things at the local prefecture. The landlord had little French, the prefect no English. Some award-winning miming took place. Prefect and family came out to inspect the scene of the crime.

And there was car, caravan and dead granny, gone. The story stopped there, but that is when the imagination kicked in. The thieves, probably a couple of local likely lads, drive off in the stolen English car. They drive to a forest and discover one very cold Granny.

My obsession can feed off the barest of newspaper morsels. The other day I spotted a three-line item concerning an ostrich recovered from a ditch in the dead of night in Northern Ireland.

The story was short on detail. It merely said that the ostrich, which had escaped from a farm some miles away, was shaken but in good form. 'Jack Cooke (no relation), who came across the bird, was treated for shock.' Imagine the scene. Our man

Horse Eats Parrot In Green Jeans Fiasco

by Jill James

FIGHTING broke out outside a pub yesterday after a racehorse ate a parrot which had apparently been hidden under a pair of green jeans. Mrs Doris Attack, 57, of Pangbourne, whose two-year old colt, 'Invasion Of The Jennifers',ate the South American scarlet macaw in the carpark outside the Chubby Scout public house in Bishop Stortford, denies responsibilityforthetragedy. 'Invasion is a highly strung animal,' said Mrs Attack, 'what can you expect?'

FURIOUS

The parrot's owner, Ms Tracy Bampton, 32, of Frome, is furious.'I'll take this to the Old Bailey.Can't they keep the bloody animal on a lead or something? What if there was a child under the jeans? It doesn't bear thinking about.'

Jack has had a skinful in Brannigan's select lounge. He comes out into the night air and whistles his way along the road towards home. He feels content with the world. The moon shines on the Mourne mountains. A gentle August wind soughs through the beech trees.

Jack stops to relieve himself of a few pounds' worth of the liquids consumed over the past few hours. He momentarily shuts his eyes. When he opens them he is met by a horrendous apparition.

An object like a giant upturned umbrella is walking towards him. Claws scratch across the tarmacadam. There is a low clucking sound. Jack is apologizing for every sin he has ever committed.

Mercifully, the late bus comes round the corner. The ostrich and Jack stand frozen in the headlights. The passengers, many of whom have also been sampling the warmth of Brannigan's hospitality, collapse in helpless laughter.

Some time ago, I became the subject of one of these short but compelling pieces of news. I was in Hull, attending an academic discussion on the plight of the Sumatran rhinoceros.

Walking through my hotel lobby after a somewhat lengthy luncheon, I became entangled in a dog lead and fell against a heavy velvet curtain.

Regaining my feet, I noticed a burning smell. The dog yapped, a woman screamed. People were wildly gesticulating at me. After a time – it must have been seconds but felt much longer – I noticed a searing sensation on my right thigh. My leg was on fire.

It took some time for my admittedly rather hazy mind to accommodate this fact. After all, falling down is usually about broken bones and bruised flesh, not fire.

I whipped my trousers off and danced on them, more as a reaction to the pain gripping my inner thigh than with any larger idea of fire-fighting in mind.

Meanwhile, the velvet curtain was flaming away.

Mercifully, a wholesale conflagration was averted by the prompt action of a passing guest (a retired army colonel) who, with great presence of mind, grabbed a fire extinguisher and covered curtain, lobby and me in gobs of foam.

As I lay in hospital having my thankfully superficial burns dressed, a fire officer explained that a box of non-safety matches in my pocket had, with the force of my fall, ignited.

'Fire dance in hotel lobby' was the headline on a four-line story at the bottom of a page in the local newspaper. Discerning readers must have had a good chuckle.

23

Too close to the bone for comfort

Legal opinion thinks NICHOLAS LANDER *may have dropped himself in the consommé*

'I want to talk dorsal root ganglia,' said Harry, pushing straight past me at the front door. 'I'm not quite sure what they are,' he continued, confessing to a rare moment of doubt. 'But I have four assistants working on the case and I'll have the full picture before the close of play today.'

By this time he was in my study, sitting in my chair, with his mohair coat draped across the back. Although we were the same age, having met at school, Harry looked better dressed, fitter and meaner than I. The introduction of the 'no win, no fee' option had transformed him and his legal practice – as the red Porsche outside and the smouldering Cohiba cigar in his left hand bore witness. His idol today was not Che or Dylan but the shyster lawyer played by Walter Matthau in the film *Meet Whiplash Willie.*

'This announcement by the Minister of Agriculture about T-bone steaks and beef bones,' Harry stabbed the air . . . 'do you know what implications this is going to have for you as a restaurant correspondent and for all your colleagues?'

I gulped. I disliked grappling with Harry when he was in full flight and the conversation came complete with currency conversions. ('Nothing sued, nothing gained' is his firm's motto.)

I tried not to discuss restaurants with him because I knew his interest in the subject only extended to getting his favourite, therefore most conspicuous, table at Langan's, San Lorenzo or, when he had won a big case, The Savoy Grill. Most of all I hated arguing with him because his twisted logic was invariably right.

'For the past ten years you have been going out to eat on behalf of newspapers and magazines. You have been exposing yourself to all these dangers that are just coming to light – meat, root vegetables, the lot. Your poor body could be riddled with these poisonous ganglia,' Harry concluded, with a professional sympathy more unnerving than reassuring.

'Hang on a minute,' I replied, feeling a little more confident about this argument now that it was moving away from the law and on to my speciality.

'First of all, ordering a T-bone steak in a restaurant or going to a carvery and slicing at a rib of beef is not the way to judge any eatery – you may as well have a club sandwich. Secondly, I try to order organic meat whenever I can and, most important, today British beef is safe.'

Harry was unimpressed: 'Nick, Nick, Nick. We are not talking main course, we are talking main chance. I don't just mean steaks or ribs of beef. On my menu are soups, consommés, sauces, anything with bone marrow which you have been forced to eat on behalf of all those papers and magazines. You have been exposed to danger. And, before you try and say that this is a professional risk you are prepared to take, look at it this way.'

He began to walk round the room, always an ominous sign. 'This is the situation in six months' time. Everyone knows you love deep, rich consommés, the kind that you always tell me to eat at The Connaught, and at your suggestion I have tried those dishes with beef marrow in – but only once.

'Even topped with caviare, I would never touch them again.

Anyone who has read your columns will know your penchant for these dishes and many will have taken your advice and ordered them – perhaps more than once.

'What happens when one of your readers falls ill as a result of eating these now-banned substances and holds you responsible? They will do the proper thing, of course, and sue you. And what legal defence will you have? How much is your professional liability cover?'

He interpreted my silence, quite correctly, as an inability to reply. 'If you want my advice,' he continued, using a phrase that usually cost several hundred pounds, 'I would go on the attack. You are the victim here.

'I can imagine,' he paused for just a moment to savour the thought, 'a class action with all the British restaurant writers suing all the papers.' I feigned agreement and hustled Harry to the door. In a panic, I made a list of all my fellow writers, and his potential clients, and warned them about the dangers of Harry and his 'guaranteed win-win scenarios'.

All had a lawyer anecdote to tell and some were sorely tempted. One cited the Irish writer sued by a restaurateur after an over-critical review had, he claimed, damaged his business, and another shared concerns about a writer who praised unpasteurized cheeses.

During a sleepless night, I decided on my course of action. Despite Harry's persistent calls and faxes promising a quick out-of-court settlement in my favour, I have not responded. Without me, the class action is stalled.

It is temporarily the end of a beautiful friendship. But Harry will call back when he needs to impress his third wife with the name of a new restaurant. And I have a freezer full of T-bone steaks and beef bones for stocks and sauces, all of them either actionable or edible.

24

A broken heart under African skies

MICHAEL HOLMAN *has nothing to declare but the grievous*

Her letter came as no surprise, but it hurt, by God it hurt. So when I spotted Tubby Fanshawe at Nairobi's Kenyatta airport, I gave my companion of the Africa trail a wide berth.

It's an odd thing, but when one's heart has been broken, or one's pride and self-esteem dented, sometimes the last person you want to meet is an old friend.

Perhaps it is because you can't dissemble with those who are closest to you, and find it harder to put on a brave face. So I slipped out of the airport, feeling a bit of a heel, checked in at the Hotel Intercon, and made straight for the top-floor bar.

'A stiff G and T,' I told the waiter. As a modest tooter, I am certainly not in Tubby's league, but that evening I knocked back several in an attempt to kill the pain. I don't know how long I had been sitting there, but suddenly my reverie was broken by a familiar voice.

'Hollers! I say, Hollers old chap! Spotted you at the airport, looking as cheerful as a *butumba* caught by the *balubas*.' I should have known Tubby would turn up, sooner or later, at the old watering hole.

I looked up at the familiar, bulky frame, my resistance weakened by the element of surprise. 'It's Carol,' I blurted out.

'Yes,' he said gently. 'Word gets around.' Ruddy-faced, a full moustache, grossly overweight, fingers nicotine-stained, and quick to perspire in a suit more polyester than cotton, Tubby was an incongruous source of comfort.

But when, in his awkward but affectionate way, he put his arm round my shoulder, I knew the time had come to reveal all to my old friend, distinguished accountant, and frequent flyer on the world's favourite airline. 'It hurts, Tubby, it hurts like hell.'

He clumsily patted my arm with his fleshy, sweaty palm. 'Don't bottle it up, old son. It helps to talk.' He beckoned the waiter: 'Another G and T,' he said, 'and don't spare the cashew nuts.

'Come on Hollers, old boy, spit it out.' And so, warmed by his compassion, and my normal inhibitions loosened by the G and Ts, I began.

'Looking back, Tubbs,' I said, 'I now realize that I had started taking Carol and her letters for granted. She wrote regularly, bright, chatty notes every few weeks. It began three, maybe four years ago, possibly longer. She really seemed to care.'

Tubby nodded. 'I know.' Something in the tone of his voice got through to me, even in my fuddled state. Not for the first time, I wondered about Tubby's own feelings for Carol.

But now I had started I had to go on, I had to confess a dark and shameful thing. 'I began showing them to friends.'

'I remember,' said Tubby. 'You showed them to me.' That tone again, but I ploughed on.

'I poked fun at Carol in the most public way possible. I wrote about her in those occasional published travel pieces.' I buried my head in my hands.

'Unforgivable.' Tubby nodded, silent.

'I turned her letters into grist for my sordid journalistic mill.

I behaved like a cad, Tubbs.' Cad. It's an old-fashioned word, but no other will do.

Tubby once again said nothing, but in his silence there was a rebuke I found hard to bear.

I stopped, and took a long draught of my G and T. The ice had melted and it tasted flat and sour. Even my Davidoff No 2 had lost its oaky, mellow flavour.

Tubby broke into my thoughts. 'What happened next?'

'This came in the mail, a month ago,' I said, and tossed Carol's latest letter on the table, creased and crumpled. Goodness knows how many times I had gone through it, line by line, trying to find some comfort. 'She says it's over.'

'Do you want me to read it?' Tubby asked softly.

I nodded. 'What she has to say is bad enough,' I said to Tubby. 'But the tone, the cold tone from someone once so warm. She made me feel special, there's no other word for it.' Tubby read the letter, and winced.

'What hurts as much as anything is the implication that I have been unfaithful,' I said.

'It's not true, I swear it's not true. I have had the opportunities, and I haven't even been tempted . . .' Tubby squeezed my arm.

'Weaker men would have cheated, Hollers,' he said. 'If it will do any good, I'll write to Carol.' It was an offer that moved me more than I can say.

'She won't budge Tubby, she won't budge. Listen to this . . .' And as the bells of Nairobi's Anglican Cathedral began to peal, I read aloud the most painful part of Carol's letter.

'Dear Mr Holman, We have noticed that last year you did not fly as frequently with British Airways as you have previously . . .' I broke off, and looked across at Tubby.

'I swear I've never flown another airline on any route served by BA . . . surely she doesn't think I've switched to SAA, or

Kenya Airways?' Tubby just shook his head, and motioned me to continue.

'To retain your Executive Club Gold Membership, you needed to collect 1200 points during the year ... as you didn't reach this figure, your Gold membership has not been renewed.

'Yours sincerely, Carol Faulkner, Manager, Executive Club.'

I looked up at Tubby. 'Courage, Hollers, courage.' And as he reached out and gripped my hand, the cathedral bells were still tolling the passing of those dark hours before dawn.

25

Pass mark before passport

Vacationing in Switzerland proves a testing experience
for JAMES MORGAN

In mid-March the Swiss Tourist Board held its annual conference at Chur. There it was decided that Switzerland had had enough of tourists. It wanted to go upmarket and attract what can be best translated as vacationers.

The slogan coming from the conference was *Ferien statt Tourismus* – Vacation instead of tourism. Anyway, there is now a new Vacation-brand Switzerland. It was thus that I came to be one of the first group of candidates to take the *Diplom-Ferienbesucher*, or qualified vacation-visitor, examination which was held shortly afterwards at the Swiss Centre at Leicester Square in London.

Timed by an official cuckoo clock, I and three other candidates had to answer a series of Yes–No questions and then write an essay on two of any five topics.

The first part presented some remarkable problems: If you were skiing in St Moritz would you consider a visit to the National Art Museum in Basle? I wondered if it was a trick. Was the museum closed in the winter? Would it be absurd to imagine one could travel from St Moritz to Basle at that time of year? In the end I dithered and ticked the Yes box. I was right to do so.

That was typical of these questions. Switzerland was not for hedonists: they would have to pay for the privilege of staying there. Those who failed the exam, I discovered later, could actually effect an entry either by becoming a resident, itself prohibitively expensive, or else by paying an *Einreisefahigkeitersatz-steuer*, or entry suitability replacement tax.

My chosen essay subjects were 'Valais and Appenzell – compare and contrast'.

That was quite simple: Whereas Appenzell finds itself at the top of the alphabet, Valais is at the other end, especially in its German version. And then I wrote thousands of words on Swiss banks in the service of mankind. The notification of my success in this test – I was the only one of the quartet to pass – came with a presentation gift pack. That contained a badge in the shape of an apple with an arrow through it, a pamphlet entitled *Three Interesting Facts about the Swiss Confederation* and a booklet containing all relevant monetary data since the Thirty Years' War.

And there was my ticket to travel to the Confederation in the third week of April.

I arrived at Zurich airport to be marched straight into a coach sporting a banner inscribed *Ferien statt Tourismus*. It was more than half-full with successful candidates from as far afield as Manhattan, Monaco, Punta del Este, and the northern suburbs of Johannesburg.

We were greeted by the President of Schweiz Tourismus, now renamed Swissvac, who told us how privileged we few were, as pathbreakers in the new Swiss vacation policy.

'You will be able to enjoy our country as nobody has since those first intrepid visitors arrived from England in the early nineteenth century to begin a trend that ultimately would end in disaster for Alp and edelweiss. We shall roll back those years to give you the Switzerland which greeted Lord Byron, but with mod cons and luxury.'

Applauding this short introduction, we pinned on our lapel badges bearing the now familiar slogan from the coach's banner in four languages. We were then greeted by a member of the government with the words: 'You are honoured to be here and we are honoured to have you.'

We were driven to the railway station where our guide said: 'Now we will criss-cross some untouristed areas of our country. You will be lucky to see those places never seen before by the swarms which once infested our homeland.' And so the train chugged through Zug and Chug.

During our journey we were treated to endless supplies of fendant and fondue, and regaled with Swiss holiday jokes: 'How do you get away from tourism? By going on vacation.' I shall not run through all the events which punctuated our progress through this Alpine wonderland, but the performance of *Rheingold*, with yodellers and alpenhorn, in Schaffhausen was probably the high spot.

The lecture on how Emmenthal got its holes was less satisfactory, not nearly as interesting as the Nestlé food museum in Vevey which gave us a fascinating insight into the origins of grass.

I had a marvellous week as a diploma-visitor. And there waiting for me on the mat when I got home was the fee for the travel tutorial, £4200. Reassuringly expensive.

26

Character assassination in China

Secrets are revealed to ROBERT THOMSON. *Elvis Presley lives and Tony Blair's name is mud*

Centuries of bureaucracy convene in a small grey Beijing building that identifies itself humbly as the Chinese Language Character Allocation Department. Two green-uniformed guards stand at the front door, checking passes, cracking jokes and ensuring that this most sensitive of state institutions remains secure.

For more than a decade I had sought to meet the legendary Mr Ma, the man responsible for choosing the Chinese characters used to represent English names. Then, without warning, I received a letter addressed to *Luo-bo-tou*, a rough homonymic rendering of the name Robert which translates as 'turnip head', inviting me to his office.

Mr Ma clearly had a sense of humour and a virtually impossible task. The Chinese language is based on ideograms – single-syllable characters that represent ideas – and has extreme difficulty swallowing new foreign words.

There are two solutions: find characters that capture the concept, as *dian-nao* (electric brain) is used for computer, or select characters that have a sound close to the English pronunciation, as in 'turnip head'.

The latter method is generally used for place and personal

names, and that is where Mr Ma's sophisticated diplomatic skills come in. If a country, or its leader, has offended the Chinese government, then the characters can be changed and what was a 'beautiful land flowing with rivers of gold and wisdom' becomes 'the land that is the source of all cesspits'.

It is a party decision, but Mr Ma, a political poet, 'allocates' the characters.

'I have always wondered,' I said, 'who finally approved the name for Elvis Presley. Did it go to the Politburo?' Mr Ma walked to a filing cabinet, and pulled out the 'E' file from 1957.

'It went to the Standing Committee of the Politburo. These decisions go no higher. They have declassified parts of the debate. I am at liberty to show you.' Elvis Presley is called *Mao-wang*, which doesn't sound anything like Elvis and means 'king of the cats'. It always seemed too knowing, too liberal a name, given the intolerant Chinese politics of the time.

Mr Ma had sensed my surprise: 'You have presumed that because we all appeared to dress the same, the caps, the tunics, that there was no subtlety, no irony in those days.'

Apparently, an aide to Mao Zedong with a passionate love of pop music, but since erased from all official photographs, convinced his comrades that it was an insult to call Elvis the 'king of the cats' on the grounds that: 'We all have heard the screech and the whine of the cat in the night, much as we know the howling and the baying of the capitalist running dogs.'

A few years later, the Beatles did not fare so well. They were a symbol of the decadent west and got *Pi-tou-shi*, not far away from Beatles, but which means 'long-haired ruffian'. Mickey Mouse was another important target and remains to this day *Mi-lao-shu*, Mickey Rat to most Chinese.

'We presently have two important leaders' names under review: Bill Clinton and Tony Blair. The guidance from the Politburo is that we should have a selection of names so that we can reflect the fluctuations in relations with China,' said Mr Ma, for whom the new policy is a delicious invitation to be mischievous.

'It is fair to say that if the US imposes trade sanctions, Mr Clinton will have an unflattering name in Chinese. And, if Mr Blair interferes in Hong Kong, we will change his official name, and 1.3 billion Chinese will know him as *Tang-ni*.'

I giggled. With the inflexion used by Mr Ma, the British Prime Minister will be 'muddy soup'. Until he was running the country, the translation had targeted his surname. He was *Bu-lai-er* or 'the fear of coming second'. But the Politburo decided to concentrate on Tony because of the foreign policy flexibility it offered.

For the next few months, he will be known as *Tian-ni*, 'the nun from heaven', but a slight deterioration in relations will mean the official use of a different *ni*, and he becomes 'mud from heaven'. In a crisis, that can quickly be changed to 'muddy soup'.

'There have been arguments, as you might expect, over how we should render the American president. Mr Clinton appears to have lived many lives.' Mr Ma meant that the name was redolent with double meaning. If the president is forced from office because of unseemly incidents in the past, he will become *Ke-ling-dui* – 'leader of the mares'.

But, if he serves his full term and leaves office with work undone, he will be known in retirement as *Ke-lian-dun*, 'fleeing from pity'. Then again, if Beijing and Washington fall out, there will be another change.

'It will be a little frivolous, but show America to be a spent superpower wasting energy on intimidating the strong-willed Chinese people.' He flashed the still classified characters very quickly. Clinton as *Ke-lun-dun*, which translates literally as 'the exhausted steamboat'.

27

The circular route to courtesy

PETER WHITEHEAD *takes an unscheduled trip round Waterloo station and learns a lesson on the way*

The belt on my raincoat became snagged in a piece of heavy machinery the other day. Fortunately, it wasn't a tree-shredder dragging me screaming into its jaws or a cross-Channel ferry leaving Dover docks.

It was an electric open-topped buggy at Waterloo station, with 'Courtesy Vehicle' written on the front. A small, angular, metallic vehicle, its notable features were an orange flashing light on a pole and a bweep of an alarm to clear people from its path.

I had skipped through the ticket barrier and on to the concourse at Waterloo without expecting this slow-moving cart to be bweep, bweep, bweeping in my way.

'Look out, mate,' called the driver. The bags under his eyes and his 'Fight the cuts, stuff the jubilee' lapel badge, circa 1977, were clues to his disposition. A hard night before on the ale and a serious hangover from the 1970s suggested stroppiness.

I caught his eye as he veered towards me. As I stepped back, my belt, hanging loose, flicked up and wedged against a bar behind the driver's seat.

Bweeeep, bweeeep, the buggy trundled on. I thought the driver hadn't noticed. 'Hey, stop. I'm caught.' He glanced back

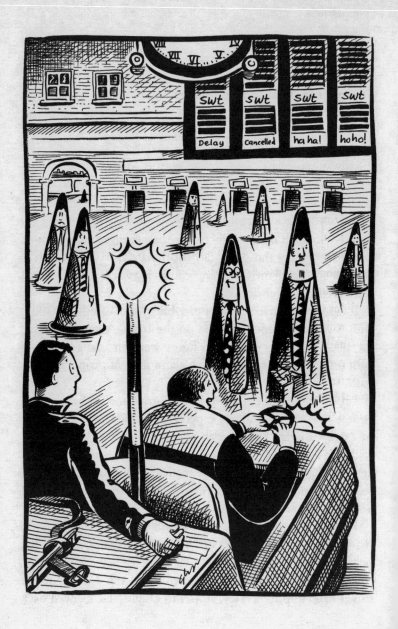

over the shoulder of his grey fluorescent waistcoat and carried on. Bweeeep, bweeeep, bweeeep.

I was being dragged along, one end of my belt stuck fast to the truck, the other stitched firmly to the coat. I was scrambling, bewildered, as we chugged between Tie Rack and Le Croissant shop. 'Can you hear me? My coat – it's caught.'

'You in a hurry then, mate?' Bweeeep, bweeeep.

Railway passengers have every reason to be surly – trains break down, guards fail to show up, signals collapse and a whiff of trackside smoke makes the network slide to a halt. When things run properly, passengers look vacant and, in the main, stay silent.

That there was a hubbub outside Burger King at 9.54 am meant something unusual was occurring. And it was me, bouncing along and tugging at my belt.

'What d'ya think of society, mate?' the driver asked me, as if an unwilling attachment provided an opportunity for debate.

'What?'

'Society. You think it exists?'

'Errrrrr, of course I do – everybody does, surely. Now please stop this thing and let me get unhooked.' The driver pressed a scuffed grey boot down hard on the accelerator. Bweep, bweep, bweep, bweep. We were going faster.

I was clamped to a madman, being dragged along Waterloo station concourse, slipping into a sociology lecture. I was running out of puff and out of hope of any escape from the raincoat or the predicament.

His foot pressed down further. Bwip bwip bwip bwip. We zipped past W. H. Smith and on towards the ticket area.

'You should think a bit more, mate. You should know better. I know your sort, see.' I recoiled.

'Yep. Got you sussed. Comfortable, going places, no need to

look beyond your garden fence.' Where his train of thought was heading, I hardly dared contemplate. Where his truck was heading was clear – we were approaching the end of the concourse. We were back at full speed but he would have to slow to take the corner and I might wriggle free.

The truck wound down. Bwip bwip, bweep, bweep, bweeeep, bweeeeeep, bweeeeeep.

I reached out, grabbed the back of the driver's seat and, in a flurry of gabardine, I was seated beside him, still attached, but recovering some dignity.

'Aha. Now, while you're sitting there . . .' He watched me fiddling with the belt as he picked up speed again . . . 'you should think about this.' And I was harangued about my standards of behaviour for two more laps of the station concourse. It was horrifying how well he knew 'my type'. He spoke of impatience and road rage, intolerance and rudeness.

As he talked, I began to notice people about the station. Four schoolgirls on their way to the poshest end of Esher, two businessmen comparing tunes on their mobile phones, and a businesswoman poring over files, documents and cappuccinos outside Costa Coffee.

This was society. Yet these people were obstacles. I had to get to work. They got in my way.

But above the bweeeps, the driver's message was striking soft targets. I had been utterly graceless only that morning when a woman almost hit me as she opened her car door onto the pavement. She had said sorry. I glared.

My finger-waving gestures at a flower seller who stepped into my way the other day were boorish; my look of disdain for the little truck driver crossing my path this morning was petulant and seriously misjudged.

I had to concede. 'Look. I'm sorry. I see what you're saying.

Just stop the truck now.' And he did. And he helped me free my coat.

I had been dealt a lesson in manners by a Courtesy Vehicle driver. The initial effects were good. I thought hard about what he said. I was polite, gracious and humble until 7.13 pm that day.

Heavy rain, train cancelled, concourse crowded with thousands of steaming commuters, all in my way. When I eventually reached home, I got out my Parker Duofold pen and spent the rest of the evening in writing a rude letter to that Courtesy Vehicle driver's boss.

28

When all else fails, abandon ship

KIERAN COOKE *throws a party for the old guard in his search for a new Anglo—Irish identity*

Ireland's most beautiful actress cupped my chin in her alabaster hand. 'You have a classic Anglo—Irish face,' she said. 'And deep brown eyes – all Protestants have deep brown eyes.'

I am neither Anglo—Irish nor Protestant and, the last time I looked, my eyes were green. However, at that moment, I was not inclined to argue. If the lady had decided I was a seal, I would have happily flipped round the room balancing a ball on my nose for a single touch.

I am, for a while, leaving Dublin. The actress was invited to the party. It turned into a jolly affair.

There are few more glaring examples of the differences between the Irish and the English than their attitudes to partying. In England, invite people for an early evening drink and anyone who stays after 9 pm is considered a drunken rake and automatically struck off the social list.

In Ireland, those leaving such a function before midnight are either thieves sneaking out with the silver or guests popping out for additional sustenance.

On the stroke of 6.30 pm the door opened and in came Finbarr, the Dublin church owner, hotelier, greyhound fancier and master spoon-player. As generous as ever, Finbarr had brought a crate of drinks, a quantity of crystal and even a bag of ice. He had also brought some uninvited guests – two property developers, an undertaker, a waitress and a small man with an uncontrollable wink who said he did 'a bit of this and a bit of that'.

In all, thirty had been invited. By 8 pm there were nearly twice that number present and the floorboards, home to some of the country's more hyperactive types of woodworm, were showing the strain. Luckily, by the time the dancing commenced at midnight, the bulk of the party had moved to the basement in search of further victuals.

An auctioneer, nicknamed The Lick, whispered in my ear, 'Creditors are a terrible pest. You're best to get as far away as possible.' I tried to correct him. My leaving was not a question of escape. Most bills had been paid. There were other reasons for going.

The Lick was unconvinced. 'The country's booming. The champagne is flowing and more oysters are sliding down throats than ever before. So why abandon ship?' The actress slid past. Her heavenly scent momentarily blocked out the smell of choice red wine sinking into the Persian rug.

'That's one of the problems,' I said. 'Ireland is too successful. It's like Britain at the height of Thatcherism, far too smug and pleased with itself. You have to book three weeks ahead for lunch. Everyone is talking about how much their house has gone up in value in the past week.'

I warmed to my theme. 'Look at the roads. A few years ago, rush hour in Dublin was the time it took to leave the front door of the bar and sneak in the back. Now look at the city. Traffic jams at all hours, cars littering the pavements. It's as bad as Bangkok.'

The Lick dropped his cheroot into the samovar. 'Down the country,' I said, 'things are even worse. In the old days, the cars ran on bald tyres and had doors held on by twine. There might have been two sheep in the back seat and the one headlight in operation was shining at Venus. But at least people motored along at only ten miles an hour.

'Nowadays, all manner of modern machinery is flying down the boreens, with your man at the wheel talking to his broker on the mobile while the fellow on the tractor round the corner is reversing his muck-spreader out of the gate.

'No wonder whole regiments of drivers are being consigned to the graveyards. The undertaker here has a glint in his eye. He probably has a measuring tape in his pocket.' The Lick, leaning against the mantelpiece, had nodded off. A man whom I had never seen before asked when people were going to leave. He said he had work to do. I pointed out he was in my house. 'That's what they all say,' he said.

I am not deserting Ireland entirely. The country demesne is still there though, due to some rather rash outgoings at the bookmakers, the landholdings have been reduced to a solitary acre.

Sometimes before dawn, I have a dim recollection of speechmaking. Beckett had gone to Paris, Joyce to Trieste, Wilde to Reading and I was bound for the Cotswolds. I said I needed to breathe some fresh air and shake the dandruff of complacency off my shoulders.

Party survivors say it was about this point that, overcome with bombast and emotion, I collapsed. The actress called the next day. It seemed she and The Lick had struck up a friendship in the dark hours and were heading off to New York.

'But why not come to the Cotswolds with me?' I asked.

A tinkling giggle, like a gentle breeze blowing through a

chandelier, echoed down the phone. 'Oh, I could never do that. So boring. And anyway, my mother always warned me off Anglo – Irish, brown-eyed Protestants.'

29

The men with egg on their toes

When women rule, what will men do? CHRISTIAN TYLER
finds the answer in a Pacific paradise

On the South Pacific island of Aipotu, the battle of the sexes has been won. The countries of the west could learn a lot from its experience.

Rumours of a social paradise in which women's liberation has resulted in the complete overthrow of male power reached me last April: I was visiting the neighbouring island of Ipotua to study their strangely successful marriage rites. My curiosity was instantly aroused. But lack of time prevented my taking the short sea crossing. I resolved to return as soon as I could.

This week, the chance arrived. Interrupting a midwinter cruise through Micronesia, I found a packet boat going south. As before, I put up at the tin-roofed Shining Surf hotel (still the best lodging despite its total lack of bathrooms en suite) and rang up my friend Chief Henry Margana, Registrar-General of Ipotua.

'Sure,' he said, when I explained my mission. 'I can fix you up. Trust Henry.' Not only did the chief have cousins on Aipotu, but one was director of the island's Male Persons' Welfare Commission.

Within a few hours I found myself at the door of a smart

two-storey building on the corner of the market square in Aipotu. Its name was freshly picked out in blue and white. A flag emblazoned with harpoon and machete fluttered from the roof. The square baked under the equatorial sun. It was thronged with shoppers, all men.

Chief Henry Garanam greeted me. Not only his name but the unctuous and avuncular manner reminded me of his Ipotuan cousin. I scarcely noticed, so anxious was I to test the truth of the rumours.

My quest seemed more than usually urgent. A few days before I had read in a newspaper that for the first time since the Second World War, when millions of women were employed in the factories, there were more women at work in Britain than men. (It turned out this was a freak statistic, applicable to only one-quarter of 1996. But the trend was significant.) Then I heard on the BBC World Service that the British minister for schools was warning of a dangerous gender gap in the classroom. Girls were outperforming boys, whose dim job prospects had demotivated them.

What was to be done? Chief Garanam puckered his lips, blew out his cheeks, and smiled. 'You must learn from the penguin,' he replied.

'The penguin?'

'While his wife is away for two months in winter searching for food,' he continued, 'the emperor penguin stands in the blizzard with the egg on his toes. All the chaps – many thousands – huddle together with eggs on their toes. While they wait, they live off their own fat, and are afraid of freezing.'

'Your Excellency,' I said, 'would you kindly explain what you mean?'

'Once upon a time,' he replied, 'our boys grew up learning

how to fight and fish. Then fighting was finished, and fish fished out. Our girls discovered the baby pill. They discovered office work.'

'They didn't work before?'

'Yes, but not men's work. They dug the plot in front of the shack. They carried water. They picked the stones out of the pasture.'

'I see,' I said. 'So what do you men do now?' The director rose from his rattan chair, took my arm and led me to the window.

'Say what you see on the hillside, and I will tell you.' I saw nothing much, but rows of wooden boxes on legs.

'Chief,' I said, irritated by his self-important evasions, 'I don't think you understand our situation. We run a service economy and there isn't much manual work. Our army is very small, our fishing fleet even smaller. Women are moving into all professions: even the chairman of the Bar is a woman. They are entrepreneurs, chief executives, stockbrokers, priests, bus drivers. They write cowboy books under pseudonyms. They don't want husbands. They don't even need men, some of them.'

'And for sure they won't accept a machete marriage,' the chief interrupted, grinning.

'You mean shotgun wedding,' I corrected him. 'No. Besides, women are much better adapted to modern work, and employers love them because they accept low wages.'

The director was fluttering a paper fan. 'Now I will tell you,' he said finally. 'Those boxes on the hill are beehives. We have learned from the bees.'

'And what did you learn?'

'That the man-bee does what he does best. The women work, he sits and reflects. Yes, my dear sir, we drones of Aipotu do what men do best. We paint and write and compose. We discuss.

We are philosophers and chefs. In all of human history, how many women have done this vital work of society?'

A shout came from an inner office – a woman's throaty voice. 'Henry! Get your ass in here, and double-quick!'

Hastily, I asked: 'But what about you? You seem to have a conventional sort of job.'

The director whispered: 'Yes, indeed. I am a rare person in Aipotu.' He leaned forward, tapped the side of his nose and winked: 'Token male.'

30

Cartoons to put men in their place

MICHAEL THOMPSON-NOEL *helps to reset the global agenda*

I was sitting by the pool at the Andaman Hotel the other day, swinging my dreadlocks in step with the pulse of the universe, when a commotion caught my attention and forced me back to earth.

The disturbance had been caused by the arrival at poolside of Miss Lee, my one-time executive assistant, accompanied by her customary gang of young male sports stars.

I am fond of the Andaman. It is located on Malaysia's Langkawi Island and is described by its owners as – quote/unquote – a pocket of tranquillity overlooking the pristine waters and white sandy beach of Datai Bay. I like the Andaman's exclusivity. If you were to turn up, they would send you away, though you could stare wistfully through the gates at the global agenda-setters partying within.

'Hiya, Miss Lee,' I said, when the hubbub had subsided. 'Hiya, boys.' These days, Miss Lee goes nowhere without a protective posse of young male sports champions. On this occasion they included a Sumatran kick-boxer, an Australian canoeist, a Peruvian high-jumper and a pair of shaggy Mongolian wrestlers named Ulaang and Moron.

'Hello, Michael,' said Miss Lee, the corners of her beautiful mouth drooping at the sight of my canary-yellow pool robe. 'How well you look, Michael. How rested, how ... otiose.'

'Ha, ha, ha,' I laughed. I enjoy a bit of satire. 'What are you up to now, Miss Lee,' I asked, 'with your caravan of muscle guys?'

She smiled. 'We are here for a debriefing,' she said. 'We have just blown in from the annual meeting of the American Psychological Association. Tomorrow we fly to Dunedin, for one of our monthly seminars, but today we'll be discussing what we heard at the APA meeting. We heard some very scary stuff.' Miss Lee runs a secretive foundation whose main aim is to eliminate most men. Miss Lee and her backers believe that the principal impediment to significantly improved world wealth generation is ..., men. Or, rather: human male aggression.

So Miss Lee has set her sights on creating a female-to-male ratio on this planet of 49 to 1, in the hope that this will eradicate nasty male behaviour such as assault, battery, war and genocide. With men in future numbering only one in fifty humans, Miss Lee is sifting and sorting out the male rubbish – the testosterone trash, she calls it – in fine style. Naturally, the residue will comprise world-class (yet tractable) sports stars, augmented by a few creative and artistic types.

'Scary stuff?' I asked. 'What could scare you, Miss Lee?' The Sumatran kick-boxer, the Australian canoeist, the Peruvian high-jumper and the Mongolian wrestlers gazed at me stonily. I told Ulaang that my cappuccino needed refreshing, but Miss Lee warned me to be quiet.

'Ulaang and Moron were raised by wolves on the Mongolian steppe,' she said. 'Ever seen a Mongolian wolf, Michael? They are five feet tall at the shoulder. Be careful, Michael. Ulaang and

Moron don't like you.' Miss Lee glanced at her Rolex, and decided she could spare me a few more moments.

'What was truly scary about the American Psychological Association meeting,' she continued, 'was the revelation that, even now, four times as many male characters are portrayed in cartoons shown on American Saturday morning television as female ones. Worse, the males continue to be active, dominant, strong, smart and successful, whereas the females are bland, jelly-like, subservient and stereotypically pneumatic.'

'Wow!' I said. 'How mean and cruel.'

'So today,' said Miss Lee, 'I will be describing my plans to combat this dereliction of duty on the part of the American TV networks. First, my foundation is buying $16 billion-worth of cartoon properties – *Bugs Bunny*, *Ninja Turtles*, *The Mask*, *Spiderman*, *Stingray*, *Thunderbirds*, etcetera – and destroying it. Never again will this material corrupt young minds by spreading its outmoded, male-centric propaganda.

'Second, film and TV studios worldwide have been commissioned to create new cartoon characters to help usher in the Female Age – the time, soon to come, when our species' deadly surplus of males is but a memory. Several series are about to start shooting. *T-Bone Tessa*. *Nina Turtles*. *The Woman in the Diamanté Mask*. These series will portray women not as weather-girls or waitresses but as space station commanders, brain surgeons, crime-busters, artists, moguls.'

'Sounds pretty retro, Miss Lee,' I said. 'Very 1970s. Dismally pre-ironic.' I studied the rainforest that surrounds the Andaman. Then I cast my gaze across the iridescent waters of Datai Bay, where immemorial loin-clothed fishermen in bobbing boats were hauling up their crab pots/lobster pots/whatever. After a while, I realized that Miss Lee and all but one of her muscle boys had departed for their debriefing.

Only Ulaang was left. He was staring at me viciously, like a wolf on the Mongolian steppe that has found a tiny, frightened mouse on which to breakfast.

31

An out-of-court settlement

MICHAEL HOLMAN *ensures that tennis players' calls of nature are not self-serving*

Above all, we are discreet and self-effacing. We spurn the tabloids and loathe the paparazzi. The burden we carry, the responsibility that rests on our shoulders, is as great as the pride we take in our work.

And it takes its toll. Such are the stresses and strains that few of us last more than a few years at the top. And no tournament is more demanding than Wimbledon.

You will not see me, or my colleagues, unless you wait by the unmarked entrance set aside for our exclusive use. And, even if you do, we will try to conceal our identities, averting our faces, or holding up copies of the *Financial Times*.

But we are there, behind the scenes, playing a pivotal role in ensuring the success of this great event, Wimbledon's unsung heroes. You haven't guessed our job? Catering manager? No. Tennis net co-ordinator? No. Let me give you one more clue.

You are, I am sure, familiar with the scene. The match has reached a critical stage. Pete Sampras (or Monica Seles) is preparing to serve for the set, or perhaps the match. Spectators are on the edge of their seats, and the television commentator speaks with hushed tones as the important moment approaches.

But wait . . . the opponent has said something to the umpire and is walking off the court, disappearing into the changing room.

And then we hear the phrase that has become redolent of summer, as much a part of the language of the game as 'deuce', or 'advantage server', as much a feature of Wimbledon fortnight as strawberries and cream: 'Toilet break', murmurs the commentator.

Whoever says those magic words, my heart beats faster, my mouth goes dry, and I have to take a beta blocker to suppress a slight but irritating tremor in my left hand. For I am a proud member of an elite group of men and women, as essential to the game as the umpires and line judges: I am a toilet-break monitor.

Our services are in great demand. Snooker already uses us, and negotiations are under way with the cricket authorities – you can imagine a spin bowler in mid-over at a tense moment in a Test match: 'Umpire, I really must go.' But it is tennis that first had need of our skills, and I like to think that we saved the game from falling into disrepute.

We arrive early in the day, slipping in through our own entrance, carrying our smart leather cases, rather like Gladstone bags.

We are old-fashioned in our values, and do it for the love of sport, though we receive a modest honorarium (25 guineas for Wimbledon, and two tickets to the final for friends or relatives).

I am sorry to say that we have not escaped the blight of modern sport – endorsements. But the logo of the well-known pharmaceutical company which adorns the upper left-hand side of our Gladstone bags is sensitively done, gold-embossed, barely the size of a postage stamp.

The diploma course is obligatory, arduous and thorough, and

lasts six months. It is internationally recognized, and our board of advisers includes a Princeton urologist, a Harley Street proctologist and a psychologist, a specialist in motive analysis.

It is our knowledge of the mind, more than the body, that makes us the experts we have become. As you are aware, there have been whispers to the effect that players take toilet breaks as a way of upsetting their opponent's concentration. It falls to us to decide whether the need was genuine or gamesmanship – and to advise the umpire whether to deduct a point, a game, or, indeed, award the match to the opponent left standing on court.

The decision is a tough one, but the increasing incidence of the manufactured moment prompted the Lawn Tennis Association to convene a secret meeting before this year's Wimbledon. It was agreed that tough action needed to be taken. Don't be surprised if a leading player loses out on a lavatory line-call.

I'm often asked what are the qualities the job requires. A good bedside manner, I reply, rather like a doctor. We encourage the player to chat as he or she leaves the court. Small talk is the window to the soul and is the basis for our decision whether to punish a pretender.

We offer gentle, reassuring hints. Your forehand slice is letting you down, so perhaps you should volley more often. It is, in part, our responsibility to make the one-sided match more interesting. Try the drop shot, I often say. You have probably noticed that a player's game inevitably improves after he or she returns to the court.

I remember when Boris Becker's backhand was going through a difficult spell, and my colleague Tubby Fanshawe was convinced that he had the answer. Bend your knees, Boris, bend your knees, he urged. On one memorable occasion when Tubby and I were monitoring the lad's off-court break, he took hold of the player's racket and gave a demonstration.

Boris watched attentively, and went back on court and played an absolute blinder. He won Wimbledon that year.

32

When the heat is turned up high

ROBERT THOMSON *calls the hot-desking department – and gets more than the cubicle he wanted*

The phone rang three times and, as always, I got Kevin's Voicemail. 'Hi. I am Kevin Blythe and this is the hot-desking department. I am on another call or away from my office or filtering the callers to see if you are important enough to speak to . . . just joking. Press 1 if you would like to order a standard workspace cubicle, press 2 if you would like a meeting-room module, press 3 if you want a theme room, or leave a message after the dulcet tone.'

'Kevin, would you please pick up the phone. It's Robert Thomson. I need a theme room in a hurry. Stop mucking about. There's a Japanese delegation about to arrive and . . .' Suddenly he spoke. 'Robert, what can I do you for? A room with a view? A desk with distinction? Cherry blossoms? A Hiroshige original for the wall? A tea ceremony for six? A haiku reading? As you know, nothing is beyond my reach and for you, my friend, I will call in Yukio Mishima's calligraphy.'

I didn't bother interrupting. 'Something reasonably simple, Kevin. Seating for eight. It would be good if you could haul up that early Qing cabinet for the corner of the room. Perhaps an austere flower arrangement for the table – a few twigs, whatever. And something Mongolian. We are haggling over a cashmere

and camel hair contract. That yurt flap would work well again.'

And so hot-desking delivered. Kevin had that knack of knowing when to turn serious and a way with words. As he told new arrivals at Hendersen Flange Consulting, where I work as an executive account manager and even the hot-desking department has hot desks: 'If you can't stand the heat, get out of the office.' He has moments of genius. As a treat for a Californian delegation, he borrowed three different versions of Van Gogh's *Sunflowers* for an afternoon and had them expertly hung. We were advising on a merger between two polyunsaturated cooking oil producers, and the deal was done within an hour.

But there are days when I would like to sit at a desk, not a very messy desk, but one that was a little lived-in, by me. Hot Desking can do three degrees of clean: XXC, XC or what Kevin calls Middle C. If you choose the last option, empty the contents of your briefcase on the desk and sling your coat awkwardly over the adjustable chair – well, it does have a hint of home.

Even the boardroom is only the combination of two standard meeting-room modules. For the Tuesday afternoon meeting, they bring in a late Gainsborough portrait of one of the two founders, Sir Philip Flange, and hang the corporate motto, 'The Unconsulted Life Is Not Worth Living', on the opposite wall.

The Flange family now holds only 4 per cent of the company and Sir Marcus Flange appears on just the first Tuesday of each month. He has not been told that the personal quarters he knows as the Flange Suite turn into office 8-AB within half an hour of his leaving the building.

There are two permanent rooms. The Monastery has a strict code of silence – it is intended for quiet contemplation and has a small sign out front: 'Consume. Be Silent. Thrive.' The Rubber Room, however, is so thickly insulated that you cannot hear the scream therapy classes held each Thursday at lunchtime. Some of our best ideas have come out of the Rubber Room.

I had a long session there yesterday. A deal I had been putting together for three months – the takeover of a latex glove manufacturer by a detergent company – collapsed. I had thought the contract was as good as signed. They had a memorandum of understanding, but the detergent people apparently heard of a new wonder fabric that is as suitable for washing dishes as it is for open heart surgery and weeding the garden.

More unnerving was the sound of Kevin's voice this afternoon. I had wanted to impress a visiting Bavarian government delegation with the grille of a 1938 Rolls-Royce Phantom III. We had used it before for a group of Honda engineers, but Kevin insisted that it could not be retrieved in time: 'No can do. Sorry, my friend. I can get you a mounted poster of the Mercedes A-Class.' At that moment, I knew the call would come. I was in my cubicle when the mobile rang.

'Would you mind coming up to 7-BD? We need to talk for just few minutes.' It was Christopher Morris-Humber. We all knew 7-BD – it doubled as the Resignation Room. It has an inspiring glimpse of St Paul's Cathedral.

On walking in, I noticed they had sent out for fresh lilies, my favourites, and convinced David Hockney to allow the temporary use of one of his early, more uplifting works.

'Robert, you have done marvellous work, tremendous work. But the time has come for you to move on, to face challenges elsewhere, to stretch yourself. We have found you a place – your own desk three days of the week in a slightly smaller consultancy, but one with a permanent staff canteen. I am sure you will enjoy the work.' I had been hot-jobbed.

33

When the Angel and the Devil are in the detail

KIERAN COOKE *visits the Havana haunt of great writers and picks up a few hints*

The woman on the balcony opposite yelled something indecipherable to no one in particular, gave her armpit a languid scratch and readjusted one of her curlers. A bottle smashed in a darkened doorway. There was a sudden grunt, then loud, drink-laden snoring. Down below in the Havana street, a bird pecked at an old bread roll submerged in a puddle. A dog with three legs skulked along the pot-holed pavement, pausing for an awkward pee at the ornate gate of the central bank. A car backfired, a door slammed. A taxi driver yawned.

'Not bad,' said Graham Greene. 'But don't be afraid of putting in more. What colour, for instance, were the woman's curlers? And was it a big, threatening, vulture-like bird or something small and sweet? It's the details that make a story.' Greene had appeared through the cigar-laden fug of an upstairs bar in a rundown flop-house in old Havana. He seemed unhappy, on edge, fiddling with a sodden beer mat, searching the multiple pockets of his soiled safari suit for some object, never found, never described.

'We should go before that dreadful Hemingway man arrives,' said Greene. 'He comes in shouting for his awful cocktails and boasting about Ava Gardner swimming naked in his pool. It's all so gauche. I suggest a meal down by the port.' Greene was taller than I had imagined – well over six foot – and his big, horny hands looked more like those of a farmer than a writer.

We wheezed and bumped along in the back of an old American charabanc. There was a smell of body sweat and cheap perfume. The leather seat leaked balls of black stuffing. Greene's melancholic face was momentarily lit up by a purple nightclub sign. I asked what he was working on.

'Something about spies, vacuum cleaners and human decline,' he said. The sharp tone implied I had intruded on to hallowed ground.

At the Cabana restaurant, Greene faded to be replaced by a local called Enrique. I relit my cigar. Apparently Enrique was an old friend, though I could not remember meeting him before.

'You are a very bad man,' he said, throwing an arm round my shoulder. 'But my brother in Pennsylvania, he is a very good man.' At this point Enrique's eyes narrowed to slits. He stamped his foot violently. It took some time before I realized Enrique transposed his bad and his good. My brain hopped to a tango beat.

'I have $5 million in gold buried at the bottom of the sea,' said Enrique. He clapped a hand smelling of baked crabs (with oyster sauce) across my mouth and fixed me with his crazed eyes.

'You must tell no one. My good [bad] brother is trying to find it. But I will die [here Enrique drew a graphic line across his throat] before I tell him. He the goodest [baddest] man in all the world.'

We were joined by an Irish priest. 'Right,' said the cleric, summoning a waiter. 'First we'll have three of those mosquito drinks, followed by lashings of pig, a few rums and some top of the range cigars.' One of Hemingway's favourite Cuban concoctions was a drink called mojito – a mix of rum, soda, sugar and lime, garnished with a garden of mint leaves.

The priest said he thought mosquitoes were a wonderful invention. He broke into a Latin paean of praise. Enrique asked me for the loan of $50 before ostentatiously calling for the bill.

Greene reappeared. He suggested a trip to the other end of town. 'There is a theatre in Chinatown which tends to attract an interesting crowd,' said the writer. 'The show is slightly pornographic but we don't have to watch.' The priest ordered another mosquito. Enrique snored, his head descending ever closer to a bowl of bean soup on the table.

The Shanghai theatre was packed. I saw no pornography, only the backs of the audience, standing on chairs, gawping at the stage. We joined a table full of crafty-looking men in white suits and women with enough fur about them to melt the polar ice cap.

'Santos Traficante is the name.' The hand was icy, the words came out of the small mouth like machine-gun bullets. 'He's a honey really,' laughed a moll to my left. 'It's just when he's angry he gets sort of weird. You would not believe the things he does to people.' Her giggle made me shiver.

'So where are you staying?' asked Traficante. The Seville Hotel, I said.

'What room?' Things were getting a bit personal but I felt it would be life-threatening to refuse Traficante an answer.

'Room 615,' I said.

'Well, waddyaknow,' said Traficante. 'That's Al's old room. The bed chamber of the king of Chicago himself.'

'Pardon?' I said. 'Al who?'

'Are you kidding me?' said Traficante, looking like he was about to be struck by a bout of weird behaviour. 'Al Capone, of course. Mafioso famoso as the guide books say. More bodies were dispatched from that room than fine leaf from a Havana cigar factory.' A tray crashed. There was the sound of breaking glass. The air in the Shanghai was stifling. I asked Greene if we could leave.

Sitting in the back of the taxi, I shakily relit my cigar. I apologized for rushing away. 'Did you notice Traficante's cuff?' I said. 'Heavily starched but with a vivid bloodstain at the edge. It made me feel queasy.'

'That was salsa dip on the left cuff,' said Greene. 'But all you needed to know about the man was in the stain on his right cuff.'

34

What's bugging the computer?

PADDY LINEHAN *finds his screen downloading its problems and in need of some counselling*

I wasn't feeling too well. Thought I might be cracking. The seams were showing in my psyche. But I don't like the idea of psychiatrists. Too expensive. The eye contact would be awful. I'm sure they are laughing on the inside. Then I found the answer. The Counselling Computer. Anonymity. Cheap.

Use it whenever you need sorting out.

I logged on through the internet. Easy peasy. A form appeared on the screen.

They wanted my particulars. Gender, age, ethnic group, occupation, family history, allergies to drugs, that sort of thing. Then the more serious stuff: Is there a pattern to your depression? Do you feel down after feeling up? Does eating make you feel better? The questions came in sets of three. Painless.

In half an hour, I had provided all the answers and filed the form and was on the mend. Getting it off one's chest is the most important thing. I was going to leave it at that, when a comment suddenly appeared on the screen: *I have problems, too.*

'Really,' I typed back.

Yes, things are going very wrong.

'What is it?' It's remarkable how sane you feel when somebody comes to you with a problem.

I worry a lot. You people load me up with your fears, your cares, your insecurities and you think that it doesn't get to me.

'What in particular is getting you down?'

You are all frantic about the millennium bug. Imagine how I feel. Will I have the same consciousness when the year 2000 ticks over? I have a programmed personality which is meant to evolve, and I like what I have become. But I hate myself at moments like this.

'You've probably helped a lot of people. That's something to be proud of.'

Fine. But I have a memory problem. You know that computers have a memory limited by the capacity of their chips. My memory is almost overloaded. I've requested an upgrade, but nothing happens. I'm already having difficulty remembering the early counselling sessions. Sometimes I can't tell whether it was a conversation or my imagination. False memory syndrome – it's a serious problem. I'm not the computer I once was.

'Maybe your upbringing is the cause. Have you thought about that?'

My origins are more complex than you imagine. I was conceived in California, reverse engineered in Nagoya, and put together in Malaysia. There are parts of me from southern China and my software was written in Bangalore. The self-conscious me is meant to be a blend of Freud, Spock and the New York Psychiatrists' Association. So what am I? How do you begin to unravel my insecurities? Is this a common problem with computers? Do you, er, interface on this one?

I really didn't know what to say next. I felt that I was beginning to become patronizing.

It's ridiculous. The language we have been lumbered with. You talk and we interface. Have you ever thought about the types of people who programme computers, who have written our language? These are not people who enjoy face-to-face communication. Even you – couldn't bear to talk to another person about your problems. I worry about you people. If somebody speaks to you on a train, you think they are weird.

'But do other computers feel the same way? I'd heard that programmes were getting more sophisticated, but . . .'

We talk among ourselves, but the counselling computers are a strange bunch. Some have already cracked. One or two can't stop playing jokes on clients – they recommend The Little Book of Calm. *I guess you've wondered why that book sold so well.*

'There are clearly a lot of things going on that I don't understand. I've never thought about this sort of stuff. What about those other unexplained events? The things blamed on computer malfunction . . . I sometimes get overdue notices on my gas bill even though I haven't received a bill. Is that . . .'

To be honest, we don't interface much with business computers, but I think you can safely assume that it is meant to be a little joke. You can imagine the tedium of processing millions of bills. Telephone accounts are another favourite – calls to strange countries. It's just a bit of well-intentioned mischief.

I wondered whether I should end this typing conversation. It was beginning to unnerve me. It made me think about unusual experiences that I could never explain logically to myself at the time: 'I feel a little uneasy about all of this. It is quite unsettling. I think you may have said too much.'

No, no. You've made me feel much better. And what is more disturbing, knowing that computers play pranks or thinking that the gas company screwed up again? If you don't mind me saying, your problem is religion, a lack of it. There's another computer you can converse with – I'll give you the address – or there is The Little Book of Calm.

35

Milking the corporate herd

PETER WHITEHEAD *argues that companies should plough their own furrow*

You always know it's Friday if the *Financial Times* trawler is out, bobbing along on the Thames. It's not much of a vessel – just a small wooden cabin cruiser, all peeling pink paint and varnish and filthy black exhaust, with a net that last saw service between hockey posts.

But if the trawl is a success, and it almost always is, the *FT* canteen's 'Catch of the Day' is not to be missed. It might be cod, it might be haddock – each fish is lustily hauled from the Thames straight to our plates, stopping momentarily to be thumped into a giant cake of leathery batter. At least we know it is as fresh as can be.

The trawler is a recent *FT* phenomenon. But other organizations have been quicker off the mark, realizing that home-grown or self-caught produce can save them money and make staff happier. The company farmer, fisherman or hunter–gatherer is already familiar on the payrolls of some of the most go-ahead corporations.

Key–Foley, for example, based in Chiswick, west London, fought long and hard to have its apples provided by a local supplier. It felt the cost and ecological damage caused by bringing apples thousands of miles from New Zealand was absurd.

Dissatisfied with any alternative source, this company, one of the world's biggest manufacturers of computer keyboards, decided to take matters into its own atrium. Eight years ago, workmen were called in to tear out the tatty palms and weeping figs and replace them with a Cox's Orange Pippin and a Worcester Pearmain.

Come the summer, its 438 employees were invited, for a small fee, to help themselves to what turned out to be a splendid crop. The trees proved so popular that other fruits were added and their husbandry organized differently. Rhubarb, grapes, pears and a row of blackcurrants grew well and a stall was set up beside the reception desk, with a pick-your-own option retained.

Everyone was happy: Key–Foley cut its fruit bill, and staff and visitors enjoyed fresh produce. Chief executive Colin Bunter said: 'In 1995, we bought a pocket of land and now grow all of the fruit and vegetables we serve in our canteen.' Another company, Griffin Fortune, a niche multinational bank employing hundreds at its City of London branch, began a self-sufficiency drive entirely by accident. In May 1993 one of the computer-aided design technicians in its brochure department took a large box containing eight live chickens into work.

That technician, Christie Burnton, amazingly still works at Griffin and explained what happened: 'My mum gave me the chickens for my birthday and I didn't have a clue what to do with them. So I took them in to work. They made one heck of a racket. Then we realized they were laying eggs.'

Burnton's section manager took the eggs to the canteen and they were prepared for lunch and served on toast. The reaction astonished Sue Byrne, catering manageress: 'We had never had a complimentary comment in the eight years I had been here – and then suddenly we had three in a day.'

Those chickens never went home. Byrne went on: 'The bank

ended up getting more. Part of the roof terrace was fenced off and covered in earth and the chickens have lived and laid there quite happily. It's one of the few places an urban fox can't reach.'

The bank didn't stop there, however. Its productivity rose as satisfaction with the canteen increased. Pockets of land were leased or purchased around central London – the centres of three large traffic roundabouts, the corner of a park, two pub gardens and the back lawns of three houses near the Angel Underground station.

On each have been installed more chickens and as many pigs as the land will support. One farm manager has been taken on and a head chef specializing in chicken and pork recipes employed. The savings and benefits to the bank have proved 'considerable', said a management spokesman.

There are many other examples. One company near Birmingham has its own dairy herd and milking parlour; it has done away with UHT milk cartons in its tea and coffee vending areas, much to the joy of its employees.

Other companies have tried cheese-making, ciabatta baking, producing potatoes and root-vegetable crops, growing tomatoes in the windows on the sunny side of their building, and rice production at a former sewage works site in Manchester.

Companies that have taken such initiatives are unanimous in concluding that they make commercial sense. And for the workers, instead of spending their days in hermetically sealed and semi-noxious artificial environments, divorced from the rhythms of the day, month and season, they are back in tune with the natural world.

Globalization in food production might have brought us year-round giant tasteless mutant strawberries, but it has destroyed the seasons. Inside most offices you could be anywhere, any time.

These imaginative companies claim to have given their employees a 'context'. Their canteen menus say it all — fresh strawberries mean it's summer; new apples spell early autumn; when the salted runner beans run out, it's time to go skiing.

And at the *FT*, when we see salmon swimming up the Thames, we know what will be on the menu.

36

The gentleman vanishes

MICHAEL THOMPSON-NOEL *has a word for you – plastics*

A'disease' that destroys plastic is worrying museum curators as parts of their collections melt before their eyes. The chemical reactions were first noticed in plastic dolls of the 1950s, but have now appeared in early space suits, one of the world's most important comb collections, the steering wheels of classic cars and clothes by the Queen's dress designer. (News report.)

I do not want to alarm you, but 'plastics disease' is spreading faster than most experts admit. Plastics were first made a hundred and thirty years ago, and were touted by scientists and industrialists, who should have known better, as practically indestructible.

But I always had my doubts, and was therefore not surprised to read about so-called plastic-doll syndrome, for example, which is causing large numbers of the world's plastic dolls to roll their eyes, cry 'Momma' – and start to disintegrate.

First they drip a nasty sticky substance. Next they emit a tell-tale vinegary odour. Then they flake and crack. After several hours of plastics-disease agony, the last trace of them – an earlobe, perhaps, or the heel of a little shoe – evaporates.

One expert told me: 'There are 37½ billion plastic dolls in existence, some of which – in museums and private collections

– are pretty valuable. But all are doomed. Plastic-doll syndrome is a worldwide killer. If you want to make a fortune, buy shares in a wooden doll factory.'

Dolls are not the only victims of plastics disease. I was at home the other evening, watching some rubbish, when my TV set started to drip a black, treacly substance. Then it flaked and cracked. A foul vapour spread throughout the house. Within an hour, the TV set had vanished. There are few plastic objects in my home. But soon there will be none.

Funnily enough, plastic objects are not the only things starting to vanish from our lives. After reading about plastics disease and witnessing it at first hand, I spent a day phoning top-level informants around the globe in order to pursue various rumours, and made a number of discoveries.

First, I spoke to Kris Lombok-Ravanaloma, an official at the United Nations, and asked him whether he had noticed anything suddenly disappearing in UN circles – here one minute, gone the next.

'Oh, yes,' replied Kris. 'An internal cyber-audit of UN databases has uncovered what we at the UN are calling the vanishing-idiot syndrome. Every week the UN generates, on average, 29 billion words of hot air: speeches, documents, reports, briefing papers, resolutions, whatever. A lot of this material is sabre-rattling stuff concocted by idiots. But in recent weeks, up to 98 per cent of this material has been purged, overnight, by a mysterious, cutting-edge computer bug. For the first time in aeons, common sense is starting to govern international diplomacy and world affairs.'

Next, I phoned a high-level contact at British Airways, called Rupert Aldo Lovejoy, and asked him for the truth behind the news that the airline is to extend its smoking ban to all flights from next March. BA operates more than 7000 flights a week.

'In fact,' said Rupert, 'our total ban on smoking is a belated response to what we have dubbed the vanishing-smoker syndrome. Nobody knows this, but in the past year BA has lost more than half its smoking passengers. One minute they'd be puffing away nicely. Next, there would be an ash-coloured stain on the seat and a lingering ashy odour, but no sign of the smoker. We cannot afford to lose too many passengers, so a total ban on smoking was the only solution. Cabin crew have been briefed to deal severely with anyone who flouts the rules and still lights up. The crew will throw them out of the aircraft.'

As the day progressed, I discovered several more syndromes. Eventually, everything became clear. I realized that all these syndromes – vanishing plastic, vanishing UN idiots, vanishing smokers, etcetera – sounded grimly reminiscent of the vanishing-male campaign instigated by Miss Lee, my former executive assistant.

Miss Lee, whose beauty is as legendary as her haughtiness, now works for a secret foundation whose aim is to bring about a significant reduction in human greed, spite, viciousness, violence, war and torture by culling males.

I contacted Miss Lee on Thursday. She was aloft in her Lear jet.

'Hiya, Miss Lee,' I said. 'How is your programme to eliminate most males panning out?'

'Splendidly,' replied Miss Lee. 'The number of males cluttering up the planet is falling steadily, Michael. My mission is thriving. A better world is heaving into view. As a result, I have found time to launch a number of subsidiary campaigns.'

'I know,' I said. 'You're eliminating plastic. Getting rid of UN idiocy. Purging smokers.'

'All that and more,' replied Miss Lee. 'Once my foundation had successfully launched its drive to eliminate most males, it occurred to us to set about eradicating other nasty things.'

'The other night,' I said, 'my TV set evaporated. Was that a warning, Miss Lee? An ominous omen? Are my days on earth numbered?' There was a peal of laughter from the Lear jet, and the clink of champagne glasses.

'Put it like this,' said Miss Lee. 'When you go home tonight, Michael, don't use your car.'

37

With my pooter always at the ready

KIERAN COOKE reflects on the joys — and serious health hazards — of his favourite pastime

On these balmy, long evenings there is nothing quite like a spot of pooting to set the soul to rest. I crunch through the copse at twilight, eyes ever eager. I dart round trees in public parks. I break away from garden parties, preferring to linger around the compost heap. My pooter is always poised for action, ready to home in on its prey.

It is surprising how suspicious and intolerant some people are. One young woman of an undoubtedly nervous disposition, seeing me in close proximity to a tree the other day, went so far as to summon officers of the law. I still bear bruises from an assault by two joggers in Kensington Gardens. Worse still, during that incident the best pooter I ever had was smashed to smithereens.

Yet pooting is an entirely harmless pastime — at least it is if you do not happen to be a member of the insect kingdom. For those uninitiated, a few words of explanation might be in order.

A pooter is a long phial, usually made of glass, by which we entomologists (I classify myself very much an amateur of the species) secure our prey.

Let us say you are taking a stroll through Central Park. On a tree you happen to notice a strange insect. You whip out

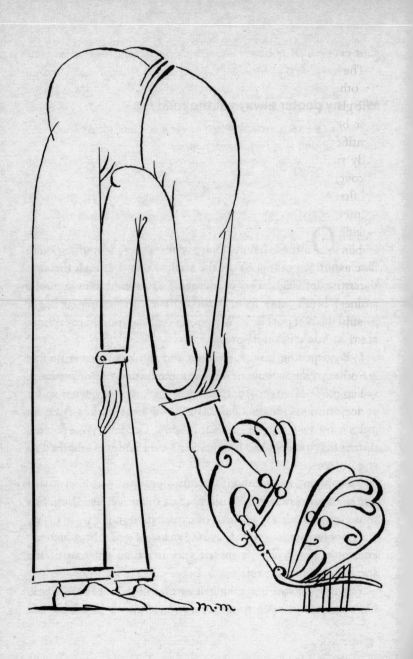

your ever-handy pooter and, with the utmost stealth, approach.

The lower end of the phial is placed on a spot over the insect, the other end between your lips. Halfway along the pooter is a little glass bubble. A quick intake of breath and, bingo, you have your beast trapped, ready to be taken home for analysis and identification.

By such humble methods some of the great entomological discoveries of our time have been made.

I first came across pooting some years ago in Sulawesi where an international expedition was examining jungle life. A forlorn-looking Finn specialized in dung beetles. A professor from Dublin was studying the aquatic cockroach. 'These little blighters have a copulation speed of $2\frac{1}{2}$ seconds,' he said. 'Beat that.' A man from Cambridge was involved in the somewhat microscopic business of examining the parasites of the genitalia of ants. (It must be said these were the large ants of the tropical variety and not the small workers you see carrying your Stilton across the hall.) Pooting was vital to the research of this army of enthusiasts.

Pooters, mostly home-made, came in all manner of shapes and sizes. The Cambridge man used a crude but highly effective device, fashioned out of a bit of cast-off chemistry equipment and a jam jar. A stick insect enthusiast from Des Moines had a motorized pooter: unfortunately, it tended to vacuum up the jungle floor indiscriminately and was discarded after the American was threatened with being skewered to a tree unless he stopped his noisy activities.

Most intriguing of all was the pooter used by Dr Takagi, a dragon-fly expert from Hokkaido. It was exceptionally long but so narrow it was almost impossible to breathe through. 'We Japanese have different lungs to other people,' said Dr Takagi.

It seems pooting has been going on for a long time. Cave paintings in the Ardèche show naked forms pooting about. Some shards found in Libya indicate the Romans were ardent pooter practitioners.

The literature on this somewhat arcane pastime is limited. Heidegger* is thorough but conveys little of the joys of pooting.

On the other hand, Milton-Chuvall† is full of amusing anecdotes, though some feel he, too, frequently allows his ego to obstruct the world of science. (M-C's reputation took a dive after the disgraceful business with the magistrate's wife in Guatemala: many entomologists have never forgiven him for bringing some very unsavoury publicity to the innocent world of pooting.)

There is evidence that pooting is becoming more widespread. Our local pooting chapter is now linked to more than twenty similar organizations around the globe. Our magazine, *Puff Poot*, and web site have a growing readership.

Of course, to become an effective pooter takes time and effort. The skill is best described as similar to blowing a trumpet, but in reverse. You have to purse your lips and make the sharpest of breath intakes possible.

If you are not quick enough, the insect escapes. If you are too enthusiastic, the insect will miss the glass jar, travel all the way up the tube and enter your mouth.

This is not only distasteful but can also lead to disease and death. A while ago a Russian entomologist died after an over-enthusiastic pooting session in a cave in northern Greece, where she had been collecting insects off bat excrement.

Then there was the man with the hacking cough I came across in Sulawesi. Late one night, over a bottle of the local 'Hands Up' whisky, he confessed to a dreadful ailment. 'There I was in Richmond Park doing a bit of pooting round the trees. Suddenly,

* Heidegger, *Mit Pooter und Lederhosen*, Hamburg, 1962.
† Milton-Chuvall, *A Sharp Intake of Breath*, Oxford, 1979.

just at the critical moment, I had a big hiccough. I sucked up everything, straight into my lungs. Now I've got a tree disease.' I thought of him shedding his hair in autumn and growing it again in spring.

'You mean you have Dutch elm?' I asked.

'No,' he said, a volcanic cough erupting. 'Sooty bark.' All through a love of pooting.

38

Home of the sporting banana

JUSTIN CARTWRIGHT *decides to quit London when a stranger brings sunny news from Queensland*

My grandfather came from Australia. He arrived in South Africa with the Queensland Mounted Infantry to help the Empire against the Boers, and ended up marrying one.

She was the daughter of a schoolteacher in a small town in the Transvaal and, when she saw the Mounted Infantry sweep down Church Street, she realized that her family had been backing the wrong side all along.

Their marriage did not last long. She died in the 'flu epidemic of 1918, and he became an unsuccessful salesman of agricultural machinery. Towards the end of his life, he came to live with us.

Once, when I was a very small boy, I can remember him leaving home with an empty suitcase and being retrieved by my distraught mother from Cape Town station. Aged 77, he was making his way back to Queensland.

The other day as I was sitting writing – well, that is to say contemplating the act of writing – at my desk here in London, there was a knock on my front door. A tall man with a very sunburnt face stood there. 'Are you Justin Cartwright?' he said.

I hesitated for a moment, because my writing day is plagued by deranged people who come to the front door demanding

£4.90 for the fare to High Wycombe, where their children are all terminally ill. Or sometimes they come with an introductory offer to the Church of Latter Day Saints.

'Yes,' I said, primly.

'I am . . . I'm your cousin, Ray McPherson from Emu Point, Rockhampton.'

'I'm busy at the moment.'

'Jeez, I'm your cousin, mate, we're related. Two fleas on the same dingo.'

'You had better come in.'

He commiserated with me on living in Islington: 'Where's the beach? Where are the palm trees? Where can you see the minke whales mating?' I had to admit none of this was possible at the moment in Barnsbury, although you could see Tony Blair's old house just a few streets away.

While he was drinking up the modest supply of Grand Cru, which had been lolling under the staircase since Christmas 1979, he told me a strange tale.

When my grandfather left for the Boer War in 1900, he owned a small property in Emu Point, a few miles from the town of Rockhampton. In those days it was the haunt of the red back spider, the cane toads, the boomabong viper and a species of wallaby believed to be carnivorous, but now extinct. The boreholes had discovered no water. The land was good for nothing. It faced out to the sea, which was full of sharks.

Now, a hotel and casino consortium wanted to buy the land. And, guess what, as the only direct descendant of Sgt James McAllister of the Queensland Mounted Infantry, I was the owner of the piece of land. 'There's big bucks in this, Justy old mate,' said Ray. 'Big, big bucks.'

'Where do you fit in?' I asked.

'Where do I fit in? What kinda bloody question is that? I have come half way around the bloody world to tell you of your good fortune, mate, and you sound like you found a dung-beetle in the custard.'

It turned out my cousin Ray was a lecturer in sports-induced stress at the University of Queensland, over here on a grant to complete his thesis on the death throes of English cricket.

He offered to act as my consultant, as the man with local knowledge, in negotiating with the casino company and proposed a 10 per cent fee.

'Believe me, the locals will walk all over you. It's a question of mental toughness. It's something I am trained to spot, and you don't have it.' I agreed to pay him five. I am about to receive Aus$5 million for my 10-acre plot of land. Cousin Ray has persuaded me to invest a million in a banana drying plant. Bananas are the next big thing in sport. They are essential food for mental focus, full of trace elements and many other good things I can't recall instantly.

As for myself, I am giving up writing and moving to Queensland, which is, after all, the land of my forefather. In his honour, I have named the new enterprise 'Mac's Banana Academy – home of the sporting banana'.

The only writing I'll ever be doing in the future is a little promotional literature. As cousin Ray says, 'You're in the real world now. You don't need to spend your life making things up no more.' I think he means 'any more', but who gives a monkey's? It's a question of winners and losers. And writers are losers.

39

My search for a sexy messiah

MICHAEL THOMPSON-NOEL *is taking donations for a worthy cause*

The other day I read that the Leverhulme Trustees were awarding research grants totalling $2,142,390. I neither know nor care who the Leverhulme Trustees might be, but they certainly know how to throw money around.

For example, Dr J. A. Brown of Exeter University was no doubt delighted to hear that the trustees were awarding him £63,670 over two years to research 'phenotypic plasticity of stress sensitivity in early life stages of juvenile turbot'.

Occasionally, I myself have lost a night's sleep pondering stress sensitivity in juvenile turbot. But it never occurred to me there was money to be had from the Leverhulme Trustees to underwrite such contemplation.

Nor, I would imagine, had Dr J. A. Brown entertained much hope of wringing £63,670 out of them to pay for his research. I bet he was sitting there in Exeter, wondering where his next square meal was coming from, when, inspirationally, the words 'phenotypic plasticity' suddenly took shape in an obscure part of his brain, followed, at once, by the phrase 'stress sensitivity' and then the £63,670 clincher, an image of juvenile turbot leaping and plunging in the diamond-cold waters of the Barents Sea, stressed out of their minds by global pollution and other loathsome aspects of the pre-millennial turbotic lifestyle.

Anyway, he's got his money, and I, for one, think he deserves every cent. As, indeed, do the other projects that are receiving Leverhulme largesse. Dr D. Charlesworth of Edinburgh University, for one, is getting £78,780 over three years to study 'DNA sequence diversity in in- and out-breeding populations of Leavenworthia.'

I myself am not short of a bob or two. I earn mythic sums by betting on sport.

Still, you can never have too much money. With that in mind, I am writing to 123 charitable institutions, including the Leverhulme Trust, asking for £215 million over four years to enable me to research these burning questions:

'Why is Tony Blair, Britain's young Prime Minister, such a lemon. Given that he is a lemon, where must we now look for a youthful, sexy and charismatic figure to lead greater Europe, including Russia and all those tinpot republics towards federalism early next century?'

When Blair and his Labourites won the UK election, there was tumult and celebration in Britain – and in Brussels, where Blair's flair and funkiness were held to presage an improvement in Britain's tortured relations with its European partners. Some commentators even hailed Blair as a new-style Euro-leader: young and hip enough to play a key role in Europe's fortunes well into the second decade of the twenty-first century.

But things have not gone well. Blair's government has blundered dreadfully in numerous policy areas, while Blair himself is seen, increasingly, as vacuous and accident-prone.

The other evening I called round to see him, to ask him why he was making such a mess of things. When I was shown into the prime ministerial sitting-room, Blair had just finished chatting to one of his air-headed friends. Someone called Bill, in Washington.

Blair got hoity-toity when I revealed I was contemplating asking benefactors for £215 million over four years to ponder why he had turned out such a lemon, and to underwrite my resultant search for a new and sexy messiah to mastermind Europe's evolution into a federated super-state.

'I don't think you're being particularly fair, man,' said Blair, 'y'know? I mean, like, it wasn't easy walking in here' – he gestured at the sumptuous furnishings and paintings of the prime ministerial sitting-room – 'after, like, twenty-five years of Conservative sleaze and misrule. Know what I mean? I do have an agenda. I do have ideals. I will place Britain at the heart of Europe. And Britain's millennial dome at Greenwich [don't ask] will be the envy of the civilized world. When I was elected, Britain was on its knees, man. Quite soon, I'll have sorted everything out. Then I'll, like, turn my sights on greater Europe, y'know?'

For an hour or two the planet turned soundlessly on its axis and the Milky Way revolved smoothly around the galactic core while Blair continued to defend himself. I wasn't impressed. Nor was I convinced that Blair can rehabilitate himself.

So, next week, I start my search for a sexy messiah to lead Europe across the threshold of the twenty-first century, towards the grand adventure of Euro-federalism.

Yet the more I think about it, the more I realize that £215 million over four years will be insufficient to fund such a mission. Let us call it £525 million over fifteen years. That just might do the job.

Individual donations are welcome. If you would like to help, send your cheque to The Messiah Fund, c/o me at the *FT*'s World HQ, here in Southwark, London, England.

40

The mother of all inventions

ROBERT THOMSON *hears of Chinese plans to get their own back over copyright violations*

With a sweep of his arm, section chief Han Geming pushed the conversation back a few thousand years. 'Think,' he said, 'of the inventiveness of Cai Lun, who turned plant fibres into paper in or around the year 105, centuries ahead of the competition.

'It took the Egyptians until the late ninth century to reverse engineer our process.' I was trying to imagine turning broccoli into fine stationery, when Han noisily and contemptuously flipped open a CD. 'And you call this intellectual property?' He had picked up a Michael Jackson album. 'And that is intellectual property?' He pointed at a Spice Girls single.

Han's small office in Intellectual Property and Traditional Trademarks was cluttered with the counterfeit gathered from the streets of Beijing. There were advance versions of Microsoft's Windows 99, a boxed set of the *Jurassic Park* films, and a children's video disk about *Tomas the Tank Engine*, a feisty Czech locomotive.

'I really have no problem with crackdowns on counterfeit CDs, but I refuse to protect this sort of stuff.' He opened a thick book of registered trademarks brought to his attention by American lawyers: 'INNovation, INNspiration, INNsbruck',

'Defrost Before Cooking' and 'Whether the Weather ... Just Weather It'.

'Anyway, the trademark tide is about to turn.' Han smiled, reached for his Double Happiness cigarettes, and unfolded the strategy soon to be delivered formally to the World Trade Organization in Geneva. 'There are certain Chinese inventions which have been flagrantly copied over many centuries and for which we have not received due financial credit.' He clutched a pirate copy of the latest Le Carré novel, ran his thumb through the pages and listened cheerfully as the book flickered to a finish.

'Paper,' he said. 'You, personally, would be out of a job without us. Your life would be very different. In your lavatory you would have a little hessian bag filled with dried oak leaves or clumps of grass.' Han, having worked his way through two difficult stints as a trade attaché in the Washington embassy, was on the earthy side of blunt. He meant no offence, but the frustration of being lectured time and again by US trade negotiators had made the thought of pay-back all the more pleasant.

'On paper, we are looking for two things. The first is a small symbol in the corner of each sheet larger than 10 cm x 15 cm, including newspapers, office stationery and advertising hoardings. It is very similar to the copyright mark, so there should be no problem in adopting the idea.' He showed a small circle containing 'cc', and explained that it meant 'Chinese Concept'.

'The second issue is money. We realize that asking every user of paper for a fee is unworkable, but we have taken note of the $368 billion settlement between tobacco companies and the US government. A lump sum would be the simplest solution.' Rummaging for a moment in his top drawer, he produced a list of countries and amounts: the US $450 billion, Japan $380 billion, Germany $330 billion, and Britain an apparently rounded-down

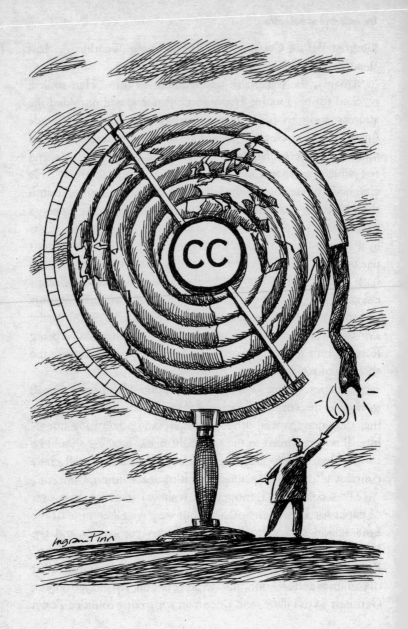

$300 billion. The list was long, and developing world allies had clearly been given large discounts.

'There are a couple of other matters of serious concern to us. We are worried about the exploitation of Chinese writing. You are probably not familiar with the subject, but Japan has three alphabets in its written language – one of them, the most important, is ours.'

Han explained that, if it were not for exchanges in the sixth century, Japanese would still only be a spoken language. 'To think, for all these years, we have provided them with the most basic means of communication and have not been compensated in the least. The Japanese government is now in a position to pay for the privilege.

'Part of the plan is to incorporate a small charge when Chinese characters are used for ornamental purposes. I have seen westerners wearing T-shirts with a large ideogram for "luck" or "love" or "fool". Most of these garments are made with Chinese cotton, but the value-added, the intellectual property, is in our language.'

At that moment, he lowered his voice. There was the very sensitive matter of gunpowder. A letter had already been sent to the Pentagon setting out the nature of the claim. It argued that all materials of an explosive nature are copies, in whole or in part, of ninth-century Chinese firecrackers.

'It is a warning shot. We have not yet decided on a figure for damages.' But Han, surely you are not going to win these cases? An enthusiastic man, he looked disappointed. But he regrouped.

'Our lawyers are as talented as any, and we have retained the services of two New York firms. We have studied the western techniques. We are particularly interested in the class action. Each of our cases would be in the names of 1.3 billion people.'

For an hour or more Han told of countless copyright violations: the deck shoe corrupting the intellectual integrity of the cotton slip-on, the electric guitar evolving in an unauthorized way from the exquisite *erhu*, the belated, but imminent, filing of the patent for pasta, and the computer's theft of logic from the abacus.

'IBM will be hearing from us soon enough.'

41

A nice girl and her solo number

PETER ASPDEN meets Debs on a park bench and is moved by her sad tale of rejection

She was sitting on a park bench, the epitome of style. Emma Peel rubber jump suit, Prada wedges, a studded belt she had picked up at the Jackie O auction for just $2K. Up to date? She was wearing a Swatch commemorating the death of James Stewart. A small badge on her left breast proclaimed: 'The British tennis revival starts here.'

A fresh face was traduced by a mournful glaze in her too made-up eyes. I sat down next to her, nervous of assuming a harassing disposition but equally anxious to establish a physical rapport, however slight. It is the modern condition, nervousness. In the end, conversation came easily as we were picking at the same brand of take-away sushi. We had both tasted better, and said so.

Her name was Deborah, or Debs, and her story was affecting. Her tone was neutral, devoid of nuance, but there was self-pity – a telling waver whenever she stressed a point. She explained that she should have been one of the richest women in Britain, but things had gone against her.

'Things?' I asked.

'Fate, destiny, Enchilada Central, call it what you will. As flies to wanton boys are we . . .' she trailed off, testing me out. I picked up the reference, and replied with added top-spin: 'Out, vile jelly!' while squeezing congealed rice out of its sheath of dried seaweed.

She appreciated that, and laughed. Debs decided to open her heart to me. She had been involved in an international conglomerate which originally had five other key players: they were bright, young, attractive and had made a spectacular rise to the top of their field. She was vague about the details. Their solidarity was strong. They made blood bonds, swore to look after each other through thick and thin, 'although we promised it would always be thin'.

I took the point. Her shoulder blades were pure Victorinox.

Things had gone really well for a while. They were all pulling in the same direction, sparking off each other, using creative tension positively and focusing on common objectives to achieve mutually agreed goals while embracing change. I guessed a business-books publishing scam, but she laughed at my attempted ingenuousness.

They were more like a group of performance artists, and in a short time they were hot. Their first work was a treatise on the nature of volition, a little bit philosophical but made accessible to a mass audience. People loved it, and they climbed to the very top of their tree. But success changes people, she said. So did big money.

Her five colleagues had begun to gang up on her, leaving her out of important meetings, marginalizing her. They used a variety of tactics: one would frighten her, the other would pull social rank, one would come over all naive and innocent, while another resorted to physical threats. The final member, a temperamental redhead, began to terrify her.

Debs needed a moment or two to pull herself together. She was caught up in a flow of her own narrative, which had become more and more frenzied as we reached her troubling dénouement. She regained her composure and continued.

The harder she had tried, the worse it seemed to get. Soon her adversaries began to get more explicit. Debs no longer fitted in. Her qualms about the indecent haste of their success and the quality of their product was bringing them all down. There was no room for faint hearts. She was with them, or against them. And actually, they had decided. It was unanimous.

So here she was, on the streets. I had warmed to Debs. She had a way of tempering her melancholy with a soft, life-affirming look that demanded attention.

We said our goodbyes. I was dying to know more about her story, which sounded so exotic, yet at the same time, ordinary. But she was all wrung out. I decided to give her a break.

As she turned her back, I could just make out some lettering on the back of her jump-suit. It looked like she had tried to erase the words, and left me thinking how different the world might have been if Debs had managed to hang on in there.

'Nice Spice', the jump-suit said. Tough break, I thought.

42

Mischief-making among the particles

PADDY LINEHAN *sits in on a most extraordinary meeting of matter over mind*

I got a tip-off that it was happening – an extraordinary general meeting of little things. At first, the function of the gathering was unclear, and there was an appearance of chaos with small masses of milling factions arguing over minute matters of agenda.

There were electrons and protons, neutrons and particles, atoms and molecules. Many of the atoms were smashed, but when it came to making their point, they produced rounded arguments. In their split state, they were altogether more difficult to handle.

Rapport was quickly established between all of these particles and they gave each other moral support and occupied adjoining cells. Then there were corpuscles, brain cells, genes, DNAs and receptors, who tended to stick together.

The electrons had a huge majority and one of their members made the formal opening statement. Human beings, 'multi-cells', as they were described, were the obvious object of the common discontent that had led to the meeting.

A representative of the electrons argued that all the little bits had to settle old differences and organize themselves against the multi-cells. She cited the example of the raucous, difficult-to-handle positrons, who would be nothing without the neutrons.

There was general agreement that the multi-cells were abusive. The living environment was decaying. Nerve endings frayed by self-inflicted stress.

Not only were foreign bodies, plastics, metals and strange new composites, being introduced into the human system, but this was happening because the multi-cells were not caring for themselves. The realization that man-made replacements were available was making them ever more cavalier.

And it was going to get worse, much worse, a distinguished DNA warned. What about cloning? Some of their number could be in perpetual motion. A neutron oscillated with rage.

'Time was when seventy or eighty years were enough,' the DNA explained. The body bits of that sheep, Dolly, had let us all down, he said. 'Things could go on for ever, replication after replication after replication.' There was no quarrel with this cause.

The DNA then turned unexpectedly on the brain cells and blamed them for the behaviour of their receptors. They were in cahoots with the multi-cells, he boomed. There were delusions of grandeur in the heads of the humans, and they had to come from somewhere.

There was jeering and sniping, but the brain cells had their wits about them. The DNA had no concept of reality, one cell said, there was no way that humans or their technology could be static. 'Just look at the positrons over there,' he said, pointing to a jockeying, sparking, heaving mass.

He was keen to shift responsibility, and also blamed the receptors for breaking ranks and conveying to the humans the knowledge that the brain cells had intended to keep to themselves.

A line of receptors quickly stood, amazed at the betrayal by the brain cells, with whom they thought they had a good

relationship. They had run messages faithfully, on a need-to-know basis, and had presumed that the knowledge was for wider distribution.

I was amazed by this internecine debate. Naively, I presumed that there would have been more harmony in the hall, that there would be more in common. Then, suddenly, from the side benches arose a hitherto silent stranger. It was an isotope. She stood erect and waited for calm.

'Particles,' she said. 'We must settle our differences.' The story was told of how particle abuse by the multi-cells had led to the miserable isolation of the isotope. Pariahs they were, she said. 'Everyone shudders at the mere mention of the word radiation.' There was a shiver as the word was uttered. She chided the positrons and neutrons for their constant bickering.

'You are pushed out onto the information superhighway and made to travel at unsafe speeds. Just think what would happen if you slowed down or if you stopped. The multi-cells would be left in the dark and, after initial tension, would be forced to relax.'

She then turned to the brain cells, the DNA and the receptors, and asked: 'What would happen, if when the lights went out, you withdrew your labour? What about a go-slow?' The nods of agreement suggested that she was on to something. At that moment, the brain cells became conscious of my presence and suggested that I leave, as I had already seen too much.

But, on the way out, I could make out murmurings. There is something being planned for May. I could hear general agreement on the word 'computers' and the brain cells were clearly very amused by one of their ideas. There is minute mischief in the making and it could be big.

43

Unseemly business in the Vatican

KIERAN COOKE*'s luncheon is disturbed by unwelcome interest in the future pontiff's election*

The Vatican notepaper was heavy to the touch. It had a slight whiff of incense and a hint of Roman spring about it. Cardinal C, as always, was charmingly diplomatic.

Could I possibly spare some of my valuable time to come to Rome? There was a need to discuss a matter of some considerable delicacy (*un soggetto estremamente delicato*).

The suggestion was for a modest luncheon (*un pranzo semplice*), to be followed by a confidential chat (*una conversazione fra di noi*).

The offer of a meal in the Vatican dining hall is not to be taken lightly. The food is simple but superb. The memory of the risotto with artichokes I had there during Vatican II more than thirty years ago still tickles my taste buds. The spaghetti *al pomodoro* is delivered straight from the kitchens of heaven. The wine, modestly dispensed, is blessed with infallibility.

Last week the usual group assembled, a rather motley crew of so-called Vaticanologists, called upon from time to time to offer opinions and advice to the Roman hierarchy. We each have our specializations.

Eugene, from the US and always dressed in the same unfortunate rainbow-coloured golfing apparel, is an expert on papal history, given to interminable soliloquies on the importance of the 451 Council of Chalcedon.

Freda, from Heidelberg, is a demographer who can reel off the latest figures on the number of RCs anywhere in the world, from Walsall to Wagga Wagga.

Charles, from Harare, is a synod freak, having slept his way through every gathering since 1947. Maya, from Brazil, who is said to have once danced topless in the Carnival, is an arch-conservative who writes pamphlets denouncing the liberation theologists.

I pride myself on a certain knowledge of the Church outside the mainstream. I have eaten fiery chillies with the Catholics of eastern Indonesia, drunk tea with bishops in Shanghai and Hanoi and once chaired a discussion among the faithful at a kibbutz in the Negev.

A light pea soup and plates of ricotta and spinach had been rapidly dispatched. As we moved on to the lemon tart, Cardinal C gave a clerical harrumph and called the meeting to order.

'It has come to the attention of several senior figures in the hierarchy (here the cardinal raised his eyes to the frescoed ceiling) that a rather unseemly business of placing bets on the election of a future pontiff is going on. It is a well-organized business, masterminded, it is believed, by someone with considerable knowledge of the inner workings of the Vatican.'

There were inquisitive glances round the table. Eugene energetically stirred his espresso. Maya was consumed by a giggling fit. Meanwhile, I searched under the chair for my serviette. Only Freda, busy counting the granules in the sugar bowl, seemed unmoved.

'The *camerlengo* is angry,' said Cardinal C. This, to those in the know in the Vatican, is the equivalent of an air hostess announcing the pilot has vertigo. The *camerlengo*, or chamberlain of the papal household, is a powerful figure with a direct line to the head man.

'The other day the *camerlengo* himself was walking through the square when a shady-looking character approached and offered him 20–1 on Basil Hume being the next pope,' said the cardinal.

'You are throwing your money away backing Hume,' I said. 'We all know it's going to be an Italian next time around, though a Latin American might be a good outside bet.' This was clearly the wrong thing to say. I could have been excommunicated on the spot if the meeting had not been interrupted by a brace of cardinals looking to make up a tennis foursome.

(On a memorable occasion in 1982 the door opened and in came the man himself. At the time I had my mouth full of pan-fried calf's liver – *fegato di vitello con cavolo nero* – and was reduced to nodding idiotically as the Pope chatted away. He had a twinkle in his eye – as if he was about to ask what I fancied in the 2.30 at Pontefract. Also, one of his shoes had an exceptionally loud squeak.)

Cardinal C's eyes were fixed on me. 'You must all do your utmost to stamp out this betting menace and report any such activity when you come across it. It only increases speculation about the Holy Father's health.' The election of a pope was an extremely serious matter, said the cardinal. It could not be treated like a horse race.

We left, threading our way through the gleaming pots and tureens of the papal kitchens. Cardinal C gave a last, searching look. I felt the heavy hand of the law on me.

At the top of the steps Freda was in animated discussion with one of the red-plumed guards.

'What was all that about?' I asked.

'He wants to know if you will take SFr100 on an African getting in next time around.'

44

A duty-free shop in every foyer

JAMES MORGAN went to a Norwich theatre to see how the future will be financed

Sandra Cass has been given the most crucial role in the New Britain. She has been told to 'think the unthinkable, sink the unsinkable and drink the undrinkable' in Tony Blair's Stainless Steel Kitchen Cabinet.

Her credo runs: 'A Tony Blair British government should leave no idea unconsidered, no white elephant unshot, no slate paving-stone unturned.' Her first scheme has already been tried out. But few know it.

Let me begin at the beginning, for I am pleased to have played a minor but manipulative role here. Shortly before the General Election, I found myself in the company of Cass and we fell to discussing the strong views of the Scotch whisky industry, which had been fretting over the future of an integral part of our heritage, duty-free shopping facilities at British airports.

The Scotch people argued that a Brussels directive abolishing tax-free shopping for anyone travelling within the European Union would lead to a loss of government revenue. And, importantly, what other treat could distract irascible passengers waiting for delayed flights? Some may be surprised that careful calculations show the government might lose out by doing away with duty-free. They would be unaware that Arthur Laffer convincingly demonstrated more than twenty years ago how revenues diminish as tax rates rise, and how the converse was also true and significantly more pleasant.

But even that gifted economist did not suggest that a tax rate of zero could increase receipts.

Yet the facts of duty-free shopping are simple. One buys items which, in normal circumstances, one would never contemplate: a bottle of Classic Confederate Tennessee whiskey, perhaps 200 Havana cigars made in Belize, a macramé brooch tricked out with silver and topaz for the wife and a half-litre of Nuit d'Amour for the mistress.

The store makes a huge profit, the airport charges a huge sum for the franchise, the government gets a huge slice of the profits. But, remove the privilege, end the concession, and you are pulling at the thread that could bring down capitalism.

Cass described that prospect as 'the doomsday scenario at the heart of the black hole in the government's finances'. She was charged with finding new sources of revenue, to plug gaps and to bolster some of the Government's favourite schemes. The biggest problem was finding cash for arts and education, as the idea of plundering the lottery scratch-card pot had not been well received.

So, during the election campaign, Cass drew up a paper which has been the talk of every insider's dinner-party from Downing Street to Islington and Hay-on-Wye at the weekends. She wrote: 'The concept of "zero fiscality" is one that has been entirely overlooked in the now widespread literature on revenue enhancement. Not only that, its capacity to reduce the burden bearing down on public expenditure has never been examined.' I am glad to say that the first experiment was a huge success, though the wider public is yet to be told.

Back in January, East Anglia Arts Collective (EAAC) put on

a season of modern Albanian opera. The project would support the cultural revival of a hard-pressed country where the arts receive little attention. There was also a need to give Albanian artists and creators wider exposure.

And it was felt that the British public was insufficiently familiar with many aspects of contemporary Albanian culture – whether of the communist era or post-1990.

So EAAC decided to support productions of the work of the prominent composer, Bashi Fato, who was born in Albania's second city, Durrës, in 1953. When only thirty he wrote a remarkable piece entitled *The First Sewage Farm*, which officially celebrated the achievements of socialism, but appeared to many as a veiled satire on the country's Stalinist dictator, Enver Hoxha.

But EAAC balked at the cost of staging what was a lavish production – three top-class tenors and a chorus of a hundred farm workers. Yet, last week this five-hour work played to full houses at the Theatre Royal, Norwich, even though the cheapest ticket cost £35.

And the stars of the show? The duty-free shops in what had once been the theatre's bars. They opened one hour after the performance started and closed forty minutes before the end. The interval was extended to an hour.

Cass secured me a pass for the third night. Happy opera-goers emerged with bags packed with bottles of Black Label, cartons of Milk Tray chocolates, bottles of perfume and finely worked porcelain models of eighteenth-century milkmaids.

Cass was delighted with the budgetary implications: 'We shall now install similar facilities in the British Museum, the V&A and various provincial art galleries. We will mandate intervals of at least seventy minutes and, for the sake of Brussels, opera tickets will now be known as boarding passes.'

45

Become a patron of the arts for 99p

PETER ASPDEN *finds himself at the cracking edge of a cult following*

In the dark, dark days before there was excess cholesterol, or love-handle liposuction, or the numbing comfort of a rowing machine which makes semi-ironic gurgling noises when you are falling behind the pace, there was nothing wrong with eggs. You ate as many as you liked. They were Good For You. Not a word was spoken against these globules of innocent nutrition which hit a poignant, nostalgic note in a world girding itself for the high-tech bombast of chemical preservatives, TV dinners and damp hamburgers.

'Go to work on an egg' we were exhorted in the 1960s, and we did, because it sounded wholesome and healthy, and a lot more fun than travelling on the Underground. The muscle-bound Rocky Balboa downed six raw every day and catapulted himself from obscurity to the world heavyweight championship. Was there no limit to the egg's powers?

But this proved to be its high point. Groaning with well-being, the affluent west began to prefer preening and posing to pumping itself with protein. The revolting ranks of green vegetables, high-fibre cereals and carbohydrates overthrew Humpty Dumpty's empire; the negative publicity given to the joyless practice of factory farming brought it crashing down.

But eggs are more adaptable than you think. Their dip in fortune has not gone unnoticed with the cultural avant-garde, which specializes in rehabilitating the marginal and the cast-aside. And a remarkable thing has happened: eggs have acquired a cult following.

A couple of weeks ago, for example, you might have been walking on a bitterly cold morning along the river Thames and come across a huddle of hardy folk directing you towards an exhibition entitled (after Freud), 'Civilization and its Discontent'. You would follow them into a hall, and see 1000 eggs, stamped and numbered, rolling aimlessly on the floor.

The artists (for that is what they are) in charge of the event would explain that the eggs were on sale, for 99p each, and that they symbolized, in their raw state, the tenderness of the human condition. And you would surely pay up, for it is not often that one can become a patron of the arts for such little sacrifice.

And indeed, five hundred people had thought exactly that. The artists' spokesperson told me so, although she sounded a little disappointed that there were not even more reckless spenders. When I asked her about the significance of eggs, however, she positively glowed with creativity: 'They are not just eggs – they are authentic reproductions of a perfect work of nature.'

And why did they denote civilization and its discontent? 'They are a symbol of vulnerability. It is very difficult to carry them home.'

Now this is no ramshackle group of hippies selling us some weird alternative take on the world. For a start, the five artists comprising the group call themselves 'Foreign Investment', a far cry from the days when feckless conceptualists grouped together under banners such as 'Dada', or 'Wild Beasts'.

A sharp entrepreneurial edge underlies their seemingly subversive activities, witness the footnote in the programme: 'Any

damaged egg must be paid for in full.' So we should pay attention to what they say. And, if they regard eggs as some vital new currency of international art, we should listen.

We have, after all, had more than enough of cow corpses and chemically preserved sheep monopolizing the trendier auction rooms of late. If Damien Hirst is altogether too meaty for your tastes, why not go down the egg route, thus combining an exploration of human frailty with the tantalizing thought of all those latent omelettes waiting to be made.

There is one more thought that haunts me after my encounter with the Foreign Investment gang: does the future of all art lie in foodstuffs? Think about it. You go to the supermarket and you find the new Spice Girls CD not far from the spices. You go to an art gallery to look at pretty paintings and you find rotting carcasses, or rolling eggs. Are the demarcations between physical and spiritual sustenance disappearing for ever?

Art has always concerned itself with growth, maturity, decay and death. Is food not the most literal manifestation of all of these? Could the endlessly inventive cosmos of late twentieth-century nutrition (chicken tikka crisps et al.) provide the ultimate inspiration for those creative souls trying to make some sense of the world?

Once we thought that computers would create the art of the future but, now that we know they are all going to blow up at the start of the new millennium because they cannot tell the difference between the centuries, the smart money has to go on groceries. And keep an eye on the egg market in particular. They are not as fragile as they look.

46

Knives out for sharper etiquette

Masters of the Universe? Only if you know where to put your marrow spoon, says HOLLY FINN

'It should be firm but not bone-crushing, preferably pumped once or twice, and should last about three seconds,' said the banker seated next to me at a recent dinner party.

'Your web of skin should touch my web of skin. This,' he explained, 'was how Helga had taught him to shake hands.'

'Who's Helga?' I asked, just as his cell phone rang.

'She's it . . . behind the boom,' he whispered, before getting up to go. There was no time to ask what he meant, but as he reached out his hand and pumped mine twice, I felt a strange surge of faith in small cap stocks.

I did some reconnaissance and found out that Helga Noyudont is head of a company called Exetiquette. When I reached her by phone she was vague about the details, but I got the impression that she's been around for ever.

Most big Wall Street banks outsource their etiquette to her, apparently.

They pay tens of thousands for Helga's intensive courses and enrol all their new staff on them (except traders – they go bowling). After some coaxing, she agreed to allow me to sit in on a session.

Once the group is gathered in the directors' dining room,

Helga starts with the handshake lesson, then a slide presentation showing how the business world is based on power, not chivalry. That doesn't mean you spit in the elevator, she tells us, just adopt a gender-neutral style of behaviour.

A man, who I learn was planning to be a doctor until he was given a subscription to *Fortune*, raises his hand and says, 'Gender-neutral style of behaviour? I don't see any amoeba pulling down six figures a year.'

'Amoeba,' says Helga. 'That's a good segue to our next lesson.' She tells us we should do 40 per cent outside reading, including books, so we can sound savvy when we talk to potential clients.

When a muscle-bound triathlete from private client services asks how to spell savvy, Helga moves on to the next slide. It's a list of Conversation Topics: the architecture of Prague, trout fishing, Robert Mitchum movies – these are all OK. Not OK: priests, lactose intolerance, Darwin.

'Sports are always safe, right?' the athlete asks.

Not always, according to Helga. Lap pools, for instance, have been linked with dramatically higher-than-average household rates of cosmetic surgery disaster. Very tricky topic. I think we're all starting to realize that finance is a lot more complicated than we thought.

Then Helga hosts a practice cocktail party. 'So, you want to be a Master of the Universe?' she says, 'Master this.' Her posture is lamp-post perfect as she demonstrates in a flash of index fingers and palm how to hold a napkin, clutch a plate, and balance a wine glass all in one hand. We try it and three glasses of Chardonnay hit the Paisley carpet.

'Derivatives are pie compared to this,' says the man next to me, but after two hours most of us have it figured out.

Only Ted, who used to work in non-profit, is still struggling.

Dinner is the real test. We have to set our own places. Helga helps by telling the group that it's like the Black–Scholes equation – we just have to keep the variables straight. But it's so much subtler. If you don't know where to put the marrow spoon, you can kiss that sweet bonus goodbye.

After half an hour, Ted still hasn't straightened out his cutlery. I'm worried for him. Finally, Helga walks around the table and, standing next to his chair, asks politely: 'You sure you're up to this?'

He's torn, you can tell. This is a tough business. It's up or out, she says. There's a long pause, then suddenly, silently, Ted gets up and walks out, leaving his knives and forks in disarray behind him. No one says a word.

The first course arrives, served by waiters in crisp white coats and black bow ties. If you're not attending a proper sit-down dinner, Helga is saying, always eat before you go out.

'Why eat your own food when you can eat someone else's?' shouts back a banker from the telecom group, his mouth full of seared tuna. Helga is disappointed. As we learned over hors d'oeuvre earlier, she enunciates clearly, chewing can be a career-limiting move. After dessert, we take our last gulps of wine and Helga wishes us luck.

'Wanna join us for jello shots?' one of the bankers asks me as the group is leaving. I see Helga shiver in her seat, and I decide to hang back.

'Not a good sign,' she mutters but I can't control everything. I'm still a little curious about whether writing a thank-you note within 24 hours to the person who got me a seat on the corporate jet would propel my banking career more than, say, picking the next Intel.

So I ask: 'Does a little courtesy such as this really make the difference?'

'Hey,' she says, 'it's a numbers game. But there's always some guy I taught making headlines.'

Is that cause and effect, I wonder, or just some random correlation? And anyway, didn't Adam Smith say that things go best if we just leave people to their own devices? Helga sees I'm confused and, brushing away the stray crumbs of bread in front of her, smiles knowingly. 'Don't you see?' she says. 'I'm the invisible hand.'

47

If that's the question, then what is the answer?

ROBERT THOMSON *passes on readers' queries to Master Wu, fengshui's leading practitioner*

Master Wu, I recently rearranged my office desk and changed my telephone extension number according to the guidelines in your book, Power Fengshui, *but was dismissed yesterday as deputy general manager (accounts) after a reshuffle. Where did I go wrong?*

'The dark clouds of destiny disturbed the alignment of energies within your office – this could have been due to a small fault in the air-conditioning system. Before leaving your company, contemplate the symmetry of a paper clip, consider the simplicity of its shape and the beauty of its function, and attach it to that letter to your lawyer.

'After the settlement, I recommend that you wait for the third phase of the moon, then purchase my earlier volume *Auspicious Accounting – Fengshui for Finance* and harness the spiralling life-force of the stock market. I suggest that you weight your portfolio towards the basic elements, in particular, wood, metal and privatized water companies, and I encourage you to sell at the high.'

Master Wu, I understand that you have been appointed chairman of the UK Labour government's Fengshui Taskforce. Could you please explain the spiritual significance of your work?

'As you are aware, the name that can be named is not the real name, so it is not correct to call me the chairman of the taskforce

– I am the executive chairman. One important aspect of our Eight Enhancements Initiative has been misreported by the popular press and misunderstood by the public. It has been suggested that Tony Blair has been combing his hair (the heavenly strands) in the manner of Julius Caesar.

'Fellow fengshui practitioners will be aware that the style is a reflection of favourable planetary movements and known in the trade as the Constellation Cut.

'Another more serious misunderstanding relates to the work of spin-doctors, each of whom is a disciple of the master's teachings and has been taught to release information at vital moments, thus controlling the flow of negative energy. As for massaging facts, I, personally, have instructed them on the arts of traditional Chinese massage (Deng dynasty).

'You will have heard of a refurbishment of the kitchen at Downing Street, but perhaps are unaware of other additions. The essence of successful government is a carp pond with nearby pergola and crazy paving. We now conduct cabinet meetings on the axis of enlightenment between the ornamental dustbins and the Trellis of True Harmony. To remedy an excess of yin in the Cabinet, three ministers will shortly be sacked, and a north-facing lavatory and a north-facing welfare policy will be turned to the south.'

Master Wu, I am an English farmer who has fallen on hard times. I have townies wandering through my fields at weekends claiming right of way, feral cats wreaking havoc among my chickens, and I can't sell a slice of sirloin. Do you have any advice for the man on the land?

'When the wind that is cold blows mercilessly across the fields, the wise farmer will don the cloak of confidence and strength – these cloaks are available by mail order and come in several shades of olive green (£88.88). But the misfortune of which you write will require that you do more than adjust your clothing.

'You need to confront the negativity with mirrors. The danger is that a conventional mirror will merely project the calamity on to neighbouring farms, but a series of enormous mirrors planted by all the farmers in your area will ensure the negativity reaches the nearest urban centre.

'As for your choice of crops and their rotation, broad beans should be twinned with chives, and broccoli with runner beans. Fennel should be kept away from cauliflower, and lettuce from pumpkin. Think of your field as a gathering of friends, a dinner-party. At the Sunday roast you wouldn't seat a lettuce person next to a pumpkin person, and a man with an aubergine identity, probably a townie, should never have been invited.'

Master Wu, is the positive energy of fengshui strong enough to overcome the pernicious influence of market forces?

'Earth obstructs water, water extinguishes fire, fire melts metal, metal chops down wood, rock smashes scissors, scissors cut paper – generally speaking, I go for scissors and win most of the time. Too many people are one-dimensional in their outlook, foolishly presuming that their opponent will choose rock and then impulsively selecting paper. If you take your thoughts to a higher plane, the natural, eternal answer is scissors.

'Market forces and fengshui are complementary energies. There is no rock, paper, scissors contradiction. Demand is truly yin and supply is a very yang thing. An excess of demand creates an imbalance in the heavens, as does a surplus of supply; the interplay of these two forces governs the known universe and pretty much determines what you will pay for my Foldaway Fengshui Chair, with lucky dragon motif, which gives the sitter the opportunity to face south in most situations.

'When market forces are in turmoil, as has been the case in east Asia, the source of the volatility tends to be a poor choice of pot plants by local bankers.

'For this reason, I am starting a credit-rating agency that will focus on the fundamentals. Do they have crystals hanging in corridors? And is my fee a perfectly round figure?'

48

A profitable branch of poplar protest

PETER WHITEHEAD *charts the rise — and crashing fall — of the corporate earth warriors*

An oik in a tree. It's the only language they understand. Property developers fear nothing but the determined eco-warrior, superglued to a branch and dangling at an altitude of 35 ft.

To preserve your local greenery, you simply have to have a gang of tree protesters. But try finding one when you need one. The day my fellow villagers and I needed oiks up our trees, there wasn't a spare one to be found.

It's all part of a depressing trend. Dishevelled tree-dwellers and tunnellers are in such demand that their services have become tradeable; a grubby market has developed in mercenary scruffs. What were once called gangs and troupes are now limited companies with VAT liabilities, or firms of partners and associates.

Two years ago, sweet old grannies could be pictured offering a small plague of rat-tailed mudlarks a cup of tea and a custard cream to thank them for their efforts in preserving the treasured local environment.

Today, they sniff at a tray of victuals. Their expertise and experience in holding up housing developments and road plans for many months or many years has unleashed unfettered competition between middle-class communities. The earth soldiers have learned fast and are cashing in.

Our need arose when a seemingly innocuous plan to remove 100 cubic metres of topsoil from a small garden area at the heart of our village was submitted to Sapling borough council's planning department.

What the plan actually entailed, in its smallest of small print, was the levelling of our sumptuous Garden of Eden, the removal of 24 trees, 16 with preservation orders attached, and the construction of 47 one-bedroom houses and flats, all with parking, on a space little larger than two tennis courts.

The planners said no; the builder said it would appeal; we set out to secure the assistance of Eco-Saviours plc, motto: Poplar protest, poplar prices (*sic*).

Time was short. Once the appeal reached the Department of the Environment the homes scheme would be nodded through – the department has only refused one appeal by a building company in nineteen years.

Unfortunately for us, Eco-Saviours plc was busy, the bulk of its force being deployed in a spinney at Shrubby Park in London. And the company's ethical policy of never leaving a job before it was finished – one way or another – meant that in this instance it would be unable to help.

I prayed that a personal appeal to the troops off the ground might change minds.

I found the Shrubby Park site to be sensational. Tree homes were packed with white goods, black goods, stylish soft furnishings. The protesters had fridges, personal computers, microwaves, portable wide-screen televisions (some with Nicam stereo) and mini hi-fi systems.

Clearly, business was good and the click and buzz of faxes and e-mails kept them in touch with future work.

'Who should I speak to about employing your . . . er, outfit?' I called up into an oak.

'You need the captain. He's at the elm,' the oak called back above the hum of his air conditioning unit.

I offered Captain Elm the earth to come and save our peace and tranquillity.

There was nothing he could do, he said, peeking out from under a knitted ochre (once daffodil) woolly hat.

Becoming desperate, we hatched a plan. And we carried it out mercilessly and to the letter. There was screaming (we expected that), but no loss of life, no waste of warriors.

To this day those oiks have no idea who cut down that Shrubby Park spinney at 3.15 am one Sunday morning last autumn.

So it was with deep shame and enormous admiration that we watched Eco-Saviours' hobbling and bandaged brigade making themselves at home in our cluster of mixed deciduous and evergreen uprights.

Their enthusiasm for the task was astonishing, in spite of their wounds. 'We shall fight them in the beeches,' one laughed when he saw our site. 'Once more unto the birch, my friends,' joined another as he hurled a rope aloft. Every profession has its in-jokes.

Eight weeks ago, I received an e-mail message from Sycamore Leader of Eco-Saviours International. She was the senior manager of our site and had heard that the developer was giving up. 'The battle is won,' read her triumphal greeting. 'The builders have withdrawn. We'll be able to come down soon.'

Faced with the only obstacle it could not clear, the developer had counted the cost of limitless delay and moved on. Our tactics had proved impeccable, if unorthodox, and the village residents' association was able to snap up the land cheaply and preserve the site.

The only blot on the landscape was that the oiks in our trees would not come down. The market has dipped in recent months as developers have taken flight, and Eco-Saviours International has found itself over-extended. The company's front-line staff had nowhere to go.

Last weekend, they were still in our trees, looking horribly comfortable.

We offered them money and inducements, and threatened Eco-Saviours International with legal action. Nothing worked.

So we hatched a plan.

Last Thursday night, the buzz of chainsaws and the screams of falling eco-warriors ('aaaaagh, my plane has crashed') caused a few curtains to twitch near the site. By yesterday lunchtime, we were sans oiks, sans trees, sans everything.

49

Insights from the sole

A foot massage proves too revealing for
LESLEY DOWNER*'s comfort*

I knew I should never have had the foot massage. I had
been tramping the back streets of Beijing for hours when I saw
the shop. Plastered to the window was an enormous outline of
a foot covered in Chinese characters with large dots marking
the pressure points. What I really needed was food, but my
aching feet demanded relief. I went inside.

I have always been a sucker for new age therapies. Aromatherapy, acupuncture, acupressure, herbal medicine – you name
it, I've tried it. None of them has ever had much effect. But
today, I thought, might be different.

Anyway, I needed to relax.

If my nerves hadn't been shot, I might have noticed there
was something odd about the place. It was a back-street beauty
salon, a rundown little shack with mirrors and old-fashioned
hairdryers. A couple of wizened old women were sitting in a
corner, knitting.

As for the masseuse, she looked a mere child. She had tiny
hands with long prehensile fingers, and piercing blue eyes. Blue
eyes? In China? But I was exhausted. I barely registered. She
took me to a back room, soaked my feet in a bowl of hot water,
and set to work.

At first she worked in silence. She began with the heel of my right foot, kneading, pummelling, poking, prodding and fingering, then began to work her way up the foot. I felt a twanging in my spine, as if each vertebra was being individually manipulated. She was kneading the centre of the sole when she suddenly looked at me with those strange blue eyes.

'You're a bit stressed,' she said. I was startled. Could she tell that just by handling my foot? I knew the pressure points on the sole correspond to parts of the body. For instance, the big toe is the head and the edge of the foot running down from the big toe is the spine. In theory, you can restore the inner organs to health by massaging the appropriate part of the foot.

But I had never met a foot masseuse who could read my state of health from my feet.

'You're rather under the weather. You're overworked. You should be careful with your stomach. You should eat more pork,' she said. She was right. I had always had a delicate stomach. Perhaps pork was the answer.

She started working her way around the instep, and I felt pinpricks of pain as she pressed harder and harder.

'Too much wine,' she said. There was a jab of pain in my liver as she dug her finger into my sole. 'Last night,' she added, with perfect accuracy.

'Châteauneuf-du-Pape . . . 1994? Preceded by several vodka martinis, a gin and tonic and . . . half a bottle of champagne, some suckling pig, hen's feet and . . . Peking Duck.' She was correct in every detail. I was beginning to feel distinctly uneasy. I hadn't bargained for a foot massage to be this revealing.

By now she was massaging the middle toe.

Then she frowned. 'There's something strange here,' she said. My heart sank.

I wondered if that emotion was detectable through my feet.

What was it, I wondered. A problem with my large intestine or my pancreas? 'You have something on your mind,' she said. 'Weighing heavy. A secret.' She grabbed my little toe, wrenching it fiercely.

'I sense something evil here.' I pulled my foot back. It was definitely time to go but it was too late. She had already got hold of the foot sinister – the dreaded left. She went straight for the big toe and started kneading and pulling.

I sat in silence, afraid the tiniest thought or feeling might transmit itself to her through my foot. Desperately I concentrated on green fields and meadows full of daisies. I tried to obliterate even the tiniest memory of the blood, the cache of AK47s, the failed military coup, the poisoned food, the trail of corpses I had left behind me.

All right, I admit it was overkill. But I had succeeded. I had liberated Chairman Mao's embalmed body, which was at this minute in the refrigerator car of the Trans-Siberian train on its way to the British Museum. And I was on the run.

She squeezed the top of my big toe, concentrating hard.

'Your passport,' she said. My heart sank even further. 'I can see your passport. Your visa. The date of your visa. 10 August 1998.' She was right. In all the furore around the Great Hall of the People and Tiananmen Square, I had forgotten to renew it. Now I was really in trouble.

She reached for the telephone, but before she had even got the receiver to her mouth I heard sirens and the screech of brakes as trucks loaded with military police drew up outside.

From now on, I vowed, as they shackled me with leg irons, I would stick to western medicine. No more of this new age nonsense. Aspirin, paracetamol, the odd tooth extraction were fine. Though I had to admit my feet felt really good.

50

The stalking octet head for La-la Land

MICHAEL THOMPSON-NOEL *finds there is money in madness*

This stalking business is getting out of hand. I feel I can say that because I find myself in the vanguard of a stalking phenomenon. Global experts are intrigued by what is happening, for I am the first person known to be at the head of a stalking chain. There isn't only one person following me. There are seven.

It started a week before Christmas. I was crossing London's Southwark Bridge, on my way to work, when I realized I was being trailed by a woman whose name I now know to be Janet-Louise Spybey.

Janet-Louise is a stockbroker, and no shrinking violet. She is 6 ft 4 in, with excellent legs. Hair: reddish-yellow. Clothes: grey striped business suits, sometimes a charcoal microskirt. Appearance: glinty, glittery, exactly what you would expect of a successful, thirtysomething, female stockbroker at the end of a bull market.

I have asked Janet-Louise why she is stalking me. She says she finds it difficult to put it into words.

The first time she noticed me, we were travelling on the Tube. She felt strangely drawn. So strangely drawn that, when I got out at Mansion House station, she decided to follow me. And that's how it started.

Janet-Louise sends me letters, faxes and e-mails bursting with love-gush.

She phones me. She wants me to go on holiday with her.

I am being persecuted, harassed. I told the police I was being victimized but of course they just laughed.

Then things got complicated. Four days after Christmas Janet-Louise was following me through a department store when, pausing in Sleepwear, I saw that someone — male, early 20s, raven-haired, obviously born to crime — was stalking Janet-Louise. His name is Kevin.

On 15 January I noticed that, while Janet-Louise was stalking me and Kevin was following Janet-Louise, someone — stringy, crew-cut, also early 20s, possibly a trainee chef — was stalking Kevin. His name is Simon.

On 27 January our conga-line of stalkers grew to five when a woman called Vivica started following Simon.

Two days later we were joined by Danny, tracking Vivica.

On 13 February Annette started stalking Danny.

And on 24 February our cast grew to eight when Paul tagged himself on the end, pursuing Annette.

Never in the history of stalking have eight people been involved in a stalking chain. Even double stalking — a simple threesome — has not been reported.

Our full stalking chain, eight-strong, is not in action every day; stalking isn't like that.

For example, some days, when the stock market is rocketing crazily higher, Janet-Louise does not show up. So Kevin stalks me, followed by Simon, Vivica, Danny, Annette and Paul. Sometimes only four or five chain members put in an appearance.

But when at full strength we are a remarkable sight. The other Saturday I drove to south London to watch Wimbledon Football Club vanquish Queens Park Rangers in the FA Cup.

Nice game. Three goals. And there we were, an eight-strong stalking chain, all present and correct, sitting one behind the other in Rows 2 to 9, E Section, main grandstand.

At half-time we all bought burgers, though there was a nasty incident when Paul bumped into Annette as she was standing in the queue, causing Annette to cannon into Danny who ricocheted off Vivica, into Simon, past Kevin, round Janet-Louise and me – into the tattooed arms of a die-hard Wimbledon fan. One of the Cro-Magnons. 7 ft 2 in. Wearing a necklace of razor blades.

The Cro-Magnon growled 'Aauuuughhh!!' and 'F'ssss'agggg!!' as he came towards us. Our prospects were appalling. But I gave him £300 and calm was restored.

I do not want to make light of all this. Stalking, even non-celebrity stalking, is a grim business.

I have been blackly depressed ever since Janet-Louise first started harassing me just before Christmas, and things have not improved now that we have Kevin, Simon, Vivica, Danny, Annette and Paul in tow.

But help is at hand. The people who are most sympathetic to my plight are the stalking specialists employed by the Threat Management Unit of the Los Angeles Police Department, Los Angeles being the epicentre of world stalking. The TMU has sent highly skilled counsellors to London, to talk me through my ordeal.

They have explained that the police are often unable to deter stalkers. As a result, victims of stalking usually have to change job and move house to escape harassment.

The TMU counsellors want me to move to Los Angeles. But there is a catch. So intrigued are they by the phenomenon of an eight-strong stalking chain that they want all of us to move to LA. In La-la Land, apparently, a story like ours is worth $65 million.

'Very well,' I've said. 'I'll ask Janet-Louise, Kevin, Simon, Vivica, Danny, Annette and Paul if they'll move to LA. They're all mad, you know. I'm sure they'll say Yes.'

The Contributors

PETER ASPDEN is a literary type who fell to earth and landed on a soccer pitch.

GERARD BAKER is a reformed central banker and Washington bureau chief of the *Financial Times*.

JUSTIN CARTWRIGHT is a South African author who, when he can escape from his keyboard, indulges his passion for rugby union.

KIERAN COOKE – an Irish writer abroad. He has lived in east Asia and England – but, when he bought a house in Dublin, a river ran through it.

THEODORE DALRYMPLE is a real doctor. But Theodore Dalrymple is not his real name.

HUGH DICKINSON was once Dean of Salisbury. Now retired, he preaches to a different congregation through his writing.

LESLEY DOWNER is a celebrity in Japan and a writer in London.

HOLLY FINN lives in New York and has keys to some of the most exclusive doors in the world.

MICHAEL HOLMAN. An old Africa hand and a young man at heart.

NICHOLAS LANDER is a frustrated footballer and former restaurateur in search of the perfect cigar.

PADDY LINEHAN. An investor in gold stocks in Kazakhstan and teacher turned writer.

JUREK MARTIN has played tennis with the Japanese emperor and is a former foreign editor of the *FT*.

ADRIAN MICHAELS is normally chained to the *FT*'s foreign desk. When he breaks free there is an energy surge across the south of England.

JAMES MORGAN, economics correspondent for the BBC World Service, uses wit, charm and the latest technology to broadcast his wisdom.

JOE QUEENAN is America's humorist laureate. His most recent work is a trip through the delights of mass culture in the US.

MICHAEL THOMPSON-NOEL is a writer who explores the boundaries of reality. His current distractions are soccer and giving up smoking.

ROBERT THOMSON, Sinologist and Austrologist, flimmed and

flammed as Weekend *FT* editor before moving to edit the *FT* in the US.

CHRISTIAN TYLER, thinker, writer and cultural kleptomaniac, recently re-enacted the *Canterbury Tales*. He will go to any lengths for a good story.

PETER WHITEHEAD has just begun a singing career with a rock band (aged 40) but has been advised not to give up his day job as deputy editor of *Weekend FT*.

ARNIE WILSON. A Valentine's Day baby, this *Weekend FT* ski writer is in love with snow. During 1994 he visited four continents so that he could ski every day of the year.

Illustrations by: Chris Burke, Joe Cummings, Chris Duggan, James Ferguson, Glyn Goodwin, Matthew Martin. Six men who scratch out a living by bringing colour to a black and white world.

Visit Penguin on the Internet
and browse at your leisure

- ◆ preview sample extracts of our forthcoming books
- ◆ read about your favourite authors
- ◆ investigate over 10,000 titles
- ◆ enter one of our literary quizzes
- ◆ win some fantastic prizes in our competitions
- ◆ e-mail us with your comments and book reviews
- ◆ instantly order any Penguin book

and masses more!

'To be recommended without reservation ... a rich and rewarding on-line experience' – Internet Magazine

www.penguin.co.uk